for upper
**beginners**

*Pure and simple Korean*

# Organic
# Korean

*Hyun-Sil Seo*

ALPHA KOREAN CLASS
Cuz I'm with you

# The writing standards of this book

- The basic goal of this book is to help upper beginner and intermediate Korean learners build Korean conversation skills.

- This book is designed to support learners to Level 2 to 3 of 'The International Standard Curriculum for Korean Language,' using everyday activities to practice communication skills in Korean.

- The framework of this book is based on 58 contextual conversations requested by Alpha Korean Class students and each unit includes the requests that begin with 'how to~'

- The socio-cultural situations faced by the team members and subscribers of the Alpha Korean Class were reflected as much as possible in the characters and conversations in the text.

- Tourist attractions and Korean names have been included to provide learners with useful information.

- The spacing was presented based on the standard Korean dictionary of the National Institute of Korean Language and the Urimalsaem(우리말샘).

- Foreign word notation and symbols were used to demonstrate pronunciation frequently used by native Korean speakers.

- Both male and female Korean voice actors have been used to provide frequently used pronunciation.

# Alpha Korean Class's Materials

- **Free audio files download**
  https://alphakoreanclass.com/organickorean

- **Free speaking practice**
  https://www.youtube.com/AlphaKoreanHelena

- **More materials**
  https://alphakoreanclass.com

# How to Use This Book

1 **The Introduction** presents various topics that students were curious about. Each lesson begins with a question, and overview of the content in each unit, including various situations where the expressions might be used.

2 **Today's Pattern** presents the most basic form of the sentence in each topic, and grammar point introduced.

3 **5 Key Sentences** contains additional sentences similar to each lesson's title. Students can follow the provided QR code or the downloaded MP3 file, listening to each sentence four times, twice on slow speed and twice on fast speed. There are no explicit grammar explanations, however, the sentences have been chosen so that even beginners can become familiar with the relevant pattern.

4 **Speak like a native with natural expression** contains 10 expressions that can be applied in situations related to the lesson topic. Some sentences patterns are frequently used in daily life and can be varied by changing a few words. Interchangeable vocabulary is included.

5 **Speak with me** is a fill-in-the-blank quiz that also doubles as speaking practice. It allows students to practice using expressions learned in the unit, in an everyday conversational setting. It is focused on provided practical use rather than matching beginner level. Students can practice their speaking with Helena Ssaem as their partner via the youtube channel. (https://youtube.com/playlist?list=PLfqI8eTWsVi6uqafGzW_qspmq1rAAnRxy)

# Table of Contents

How to study with Alpha Korean Class
Tips On Using This Book

## Unit 3    Transport & Directions

## Unit 4    Emergencies

## Unit 8　Everyday life

# UNIT 1

# Food & Dining

TRACK 1

# 아이스아메리카노 주세요.
## Can I get an iced Americano?

 **Do you want to know** How to order coffee at a café?

It's easy: say ~주세요. You just need to mention the item you want to order before 주세요. By adding 하나 after the name of the item, you can order one of anything using the pattern ~하나 주세요. In everyday speech, we say 주세요 without the 을/를 object particles: generally, particles are not frequently used in everyday spoken Korean.

### Today's Pattern

| N | 주세요 |
|---|---|
| **아이스아메리카노** | **주세요** |
| **an iced Americano** | **Can I get** |

**Can I get an iced Americano?**
~주세요

### 5 Key Sentences

- **아이스아메리카노 주세요.** — Can I get an iced Americano?
- **따뜻한 카페라테 주세요.**
  [따뜨탄] — Can I get a hot café latte?
- **따뜻한 바닐라라테 주세요.** — Can I get a hot vanilla latte?
- **아이스아인슈페너 주세요.** — Can I get an iced Einspänner?
  ▶ Einspanner is a coffee drink that is popular in Korea but originates from Vienna, Austria.
- **그린티프라푸치노 주세요.** — Can I get a green tea Frappuccino?

10

**Speak like a native with natural expressions**

**Tall size, please**

**톨 사이즈로 주세요.**

▸ **스몰 사이즈** small size
▸ **라지 사이즈** large size
▸ **그란데 사이즈** grande size

● When talking about sizes, try to use the pattern '(사이즈)~로 주세요.'

**I'd also like a chocolate cake.**

**초콜릿케이크도 주세요.**

▸ **브라우니** brownies
▸ **베이글** bagel

● If you want to order more items besides your drink, use '~도 주세요'

**Give me some water, please**

**물 좀 주세요.**

▸ **영수증** a receipt
▸ **티슈** tissue

● '~ 좀 주세요' It's a gentle expression than just '주세요' to ask for something.

**I'd like it to go.**

**포장해 주세요.**

▸ **테이크아웃** take-out, takeaway, to go

● 포장하다 to wrap

**Lots of ice, please.**

**얼음 많이 넣어 주세요.**
[어름 마니]

▸ **넣다** put in

**Just a little whipped cream, please.**

**휘핑크림 조금만 넣어 주세요.**

● 조금 a little, 만 only

**I'd like a loyalty card, please.**

포인트 카드 만들어 주세요. 🔊
[만드러]

● 만들다 to make

**Can I have low-fat milk instead?**

저지방 우유로 바꿔 주세요. 🔊

▶ **두유** soy milk

▶ **무지방 우유** skim milk

● 바꾸다 to change, to exchange

**Make it a double shot, please.**

샷 추가해 주세요. 🔊

● 추가하다 to add

**No whipped cream, please.**

휘핑크림 빼 주세요. 🔊

● 빼다 hold

Write down the appropriate sentence in the blank space and practice your pronunciations by reading out loud.

**Employee** 주문하시겠어요?
Would you like to order?

**Seohyeon** _____ ❶
Can I get an iced café latte?

**Employee** 네, 무슨 사이즈로 드릴까요?
What size would you like?

**Seohyeon** _____ ❷
Tall size, please.

**Employee** 네, 매장에서 드시나요?
Sure, for here?

**Seohyeon** _____ ❸
No, I'd like it to go.

---

**Answer**

❶ Can I get an iced café latte?  아이스카페라테 하나 주세요.
❷ Tall size, please.  톨 사이즈로 주세요.
❸ No, I'd like it to go.  아니요. 포장해 주세요 (테이크아웃해 주세요)

13

TRACK 3

# 떡볶이랑 순대 주세요.
## Can I get the Tteokbokki and Sundae?

 **Do you want to know** How to order food at a restaurant?

At a restaurant, Koreans usually love to order several items on the menu and share the food with others. You may also want to order lots of different food and drinks.

At such times, you can use the pattern ~랑/이랑 ~주세요 to order the things you want. Just like in the word '떡볶이', if there is no ending consonant (받침), you should use ~랑. If there is an ending consonant, like in '김밥', then use ~이랑 after the word. Like this, you can connect two or more items on the menu while ordering. Ordering everything you want at once is easier, isn't it?

---

**Today's Pattern**

| N1+랑/이랑+N2 | 주세요 |
|---|---|
| **떡볶이랑 순대** | **주세요** |
| the Tteokbokki and Sundae | Can I get |

**Can I get the Tteokbokki and Sundae?**
~랑/이랑 ~주세요.

---

**5 Key** **Sentences**

- **떡볶이랑 순대 주세요.**    Can I get the Tteokbokki and Sundae?
- **짜장면이랑 짬뽕 주세요.**    Can I get the Black Bean Sauce Noodles and Spicy Seafood Noodle Soup?
- **물냉면이랑 고기만두 주세요.**    Can I get the Cold Buckwheat Noodles and Meat Mandu?
- **육회비빔밥이랑 산낙지 주세요.**    Can I get the Beef Tartare Bibimbap and the Sliced Live Octopus?
  [비빔빱]     [산낙찌]

**Speak like a native with natural expressions**

**One Tteokbokki and one fried squid, please.**

떡볶이 하나랑 오징어튀김 하나 주세요. 📢
[떡뽀끼]

▸ **김말이** Deep-fried Laver Roll
▸ **야채튀김** Deep-fried Vegetables

**Two servings of Grilled Pork Belly and a bottle of soju, please.**

삼겹살 2인분이랑 소주 한 병 주세요. 📢
[삼겹쌀]　　　　　　　　[쏘주]

▸ **1인분** 1 serving
▸ **3인분** 3 servings

**I'd like to have a Seafood and Green Onion Pancake and a bottle of Unrefined Rice Wine, please.**

해물파전 하나랑 막걸리 한 병 주세요. 📢

▸ **맥주 한 병** a bottle of beer

**Mr, I need two individual plates here, please.**

사장님, 여기 앞접시 두 개 주세요. 📢
[압쩝씨]

● Plates that are used for sharing food are called '앞접시'

**Ma'am, please give me more kimchi.**

사장님, 김치 좀 더 주세요. 📢

▸ **반찬** banchan

**One more spoon, please.**

숟가락 하나 더 주세요. 📢
[숟까락]

▸ **젓가락** chopsticks
▸ **포크** fork

**Can I have the menu, please?**　메뉴판 좀 주세요. 📢

**One fried chicken and two pints of beer, please.**

**프라이드치킨 한 마리랑 500 두 잔 주세요.** 🔊

- 500=500cc=500ml beer
- Asking for "two pints of beer" is the same as asking for two 500ml servings of beer. You can often see this at Korean pubs that serve chicken and beer on tap.

**I'd like this to go, please.**

**이거 포장해 주세요.** 🔊

**Can you get me some iced water, please?**

**얼음물 좀 갖다주세요.** 🔊

▷ **앞치마** apron
- When you're worried about food splashing, especially if you're wearing white, ask for an apron at the restaurant.

Write down the appropriate sentence in the blank space and practice your pronunciations by reading out loud.

**Employee**  주문하시겠어요?
What can I get for you?

**Minjun**  _____ ❶
Three servings of pork belly and a bottle of soju, please.

**Employee**  네, 무슨 소주로 드릴까요?

**Minjun**  _____ ❶
Chamisul, please.

**Employee**  잔은 몇 개 드릴까요?
How many glasses would you like?

**Minjun**  _____ ❶
Give me two

- 참이슬 (Chamisul) is a brand of soju. 참이슬, along with the brand 처음처럼, are very well-known in Korea.

**Answer**

❶ Three servings of pork belly and a bottle of soju, please.
삼겹살 3인분이랑 소주 한 병 주세요.
❷ Chamisul, please.  참이슬로 주세요.
❸ Give me two.  두 개 주세요.

17

TRACK 5

# 여기 땅콩이 들어가나요?
**Does this dish have peanuts in it?**

 **Do you want to know How to ask if a dish has an ingredient that you are allergic to?**

For those who have nuts or seafood allergies, trying new food for the first time can be worrying, can't it? Worry not, you can use this sentence pattern to check if a dish contains ingredients you cannot eat, such as peanuts, milk, eggs, etc.

---

**Today's Pattern**

| 여기 | N+이/가 | 들어가나요? |
|---|---|---|
| **여기** | **땅콩이** | **들어가나요?** |
| in this food | peanuts | have |

**Does this dish have peanuts in it?**
여기 ~이/가 들어가나요?

---

**5 Key Sentences**

- **여기 땅콩이 들어가나요?**　　Does this dish have peanuts in it?
  [드러가나요]
- **여기 계란이 들어가나요?**　　Does this food have eggs in it?
- **여기 우유가 들어가나요?**　　Does this dish have milk in it?
- **여기 뭐가 들어가나요?**　　What does this dish/food have in it?
- **여기 오이가 들어가나요?**　　Does this food have cucumbers in it?

## Speak like a native with natural expressions

**I'm allergic to nuts.**

저는 견과류 알레르기가 있어요. 🔊

▹ **새우** shrimp
▹ **복숭아** peach

**I'm a vegetarian.**

저는 채식주의자예요. 🔊

▹ **비건** vegan
● In Korea, the term 'vegan' is not yet widespread. Because the concept is still new to many, you have to specifically say that you cannot eat eggs and milk.

**I can't eat peanuts.**

저는 땅콩을 못 먹어요. 🔊
[몬 머거요]

▹ **아몬드** almonds
▹ **호두** walnuts

**I can't eat things like this.**

이런 거 못 먹어요. 🔊
[이렁 거]

**I can't handle spicy food.**

저는 매운 걸 못 먹어요. 🔊

▹ **단 걸** sweet food

**What's in it?**

이 안에 뭐가 들어가요? 🔊

**Please make it not spicy.**

안 맵게 해 주세요. 🔊

▹ **안 달게** not sweet
▹ **안 짜게** not salty

**Please hold the eggs.**

계란은 빼 주세요. 🔊

● For words that have ending consonants (받침), just like the '란' in 계란, we use the particle '은'. It is still correct without the particle, such as '계란 빼 주세요'. Using '은', however, can be used for emphasis, implying that "everything else is fine, but eggs".

**I'd like to have it without cucumbers.**

그럼, 오이는 빼고 주세요. ◁╳

● For words that do not have 받침, like the '이' in '오이', we add the particle '는' at the end.

**I sneeze when I eat things like this.**

이런 거 먹으면 재채기가 나요. ◁╳

▷ **콧물(이)** runny nose
▷ **두드러기(가)** hives

Write down the appropriate sentence in the blank space and practice your pronunciations by reading out loud.

---

**Sooah**   저기요, _____? ❶
Excuse me, what's in this dish?

**Employee**   콩나물이랑 당근, 버섯 그리고 시금치, 소고기, 계란이 들어갑니다.
It has bean sprouts, carrots, mushrooms, spinach, beef, and eggs

**Sooah**   아, 그럼, _____? ❷
Oh, then it doesn't have cucumber in it?

**Employee**   아, 오이도 들어가요.
Ah, there are cucumbers in it, too.

**Sooah**   _____ ❸
I'd like to have it without cucumbers.

---

**Employee**   알겠습니다.
Alright.

---

### Answer

❶ What's in this dish?                          여기에 뭐가 들어가요?
❷ it doesn't have cucumber in it?              여기에 오이는 안 들어가나요?
❸ I'd like to have it without cucumbers.       그럼, 오이는 빼고 주세요.

TRACK 7

# 비건 추천 메뉴 있나요?
**Do you have any vegan recommendations?**

 **Do you want to know How to ask if there is a vegan menu?**

If you are a vegan, you may feel the need to watch out for the non-vegan ingredients added in a meal when eating in Korea. At times, it can be a challenge to find vegan dishes. Wouldn't it be nice to ask only one question to resolve the issue? Good news! There is one question that does just that: Do you have any vegan recommendations? Currently, the number of vegan products in Korea is increasing, but there are still many people who have no idea what "vegan" means. So, for vegans who have plans to visit Korea, I recommend you search #비건식당 (#vegan-restaurant) on Instagram, and find out which restaurants you can eat at.

## Today's Pattern

| N | 추천 메뉴 | 있나요? |
|---|---|---|
| **비건** | **추천 메뉴** | **있나요?** |
| vegan | recommendations | Do you have |

**Do you have any vegan recommendations?**
~추천 메뉴 있나요?

## 5 Key Sentences

- 비건 추천 메뉴 있나요? — Do you have any vegan recommendations?
- 어린이 추천 메뉴 있나요? — Do you have a kids' menu?
- 브런치 추천 메뉴 있나요? — Do you have a brunch menu?
- 점심 추천 메뉴 있나요? — Do you have any lunch recommendations?
- 저녁 추천 메뉴 있나요? — Do you have any dinner recommendations?

**Speak like a native with natural expressions**

| | |
|---|---|
| **Do you have any other recommendations besides coffee?** | 혹시, 커피 말고 추천 메뉴 있나요? 🔊<br><br>▸ **고기** meat<br>▸ **한식** Korean food |
| **I'm looking for a vegan menu.** | 저는 비건 메뉴를 찾고 있어요. 🔊 |
| **Please recommend a food that is good for digestion.** | 소화가 잘 되는 음식으로 추천해 주세요. 🔊<br>[추처내] |
| **Please recommend Gangwon-do's signature food.** | 강원도 대표 음식을 추천해 주세요. 🔊<br><br>▸ **이 지역** this region |
| **It's my first time here, do you have any recommendations?** | 여기 처음인데, 추천 메뉴 있나요? 🔊 |
| **What's good in Jeju Island?** | 제주도에서는 뭐가 맛있어요? 🔊 |
| **Please recommend a must-go restaurant in Gangnam.** | 강남 맛집 추천해 주세요. 🔊<br><br>▸ **홍대** Hongdae<br>▸ **성수** Seongsu<br><br>● "맛집" is short for '맛있는 집', and means 'delicious restaurant'. |
| **Do you know a good restaurant for a solo dinner?** | 혼자 갈 만한 맛집 있을까요? 🔊<br><br>▸ **가족끼리 갈 만한** family-friendly<br>▸ **아이와 갈 만한** kid-friendly<br>▸ **커플이 갈 만한** good for couples to go to |

**23**

**Please recommend a non-spicy chicken (dish).**    안 매운 치킨 추천해 주세요. 🔊

**What's the best thing to buy at a convenience store?**    편의점 추천 메뉴 좀 알려 주세요. 🔊
[펴니점]

▶ **찜질방** Korean sauna

Write down the appropriate sentence in the blank space and practice your pronunciations by reading out loud.

**Employee**　주문하시겠어요?

May I take your order?

**Seohyeon**　_____ ❶

It's my first time here, do you have any recommendations?

**Employee**　네, 칠리베이컨 웜볼이 제일 잘 나가요.

Sure, the chilli bacon warm bowl (dish) is the best.

**Seohyeon**　그거 말고, _____ ❷

Besides that, do you have any vegan recommendations?

**Employee**　비건 메뉴는 고추장 머쉬룸 웜볼이 잘 나가요.

For the vegan menu, the red pepper paste mushroom warm balls (dish) are popular.

**Seohyeon**　죄송한데, _____ ❸

I'm sorry, but please recommend something that's not spicy.

### Answer

❶ It's my first time here, do you have any recommendations?
여기 처음인데, 추천 메뉴 있나요?
❷ Do you have any vegan recommendations?　비건 추천 메뉴 있나요?
❸ Please recommend something that's not spicy.　안 매운 걸로 추천해 주세요.

25

# 제일 인기 있는 메뉴가 뭐예요?
## What's your most popular dish?

 **Do you want to know** How to ask for a restaurant's most popular dish?

Are you adventurous? Then, when you go to a restaurant for the first time, you would want to try dishes that Koreans enjoy as well. However, you wouldn't know the popular dishes when you look on the menu with unfamiliar names for the first time. It situations like this, simply ask this question: "제일 인기 있는 메뉴가 뭐예요?" What is your most popular dish? This way, you can conveniently try the local favourites.

### Today's Pattern

| 제일/가장 인기 있는 | N+이/가 | 뭐예요? |
|---|---|---|
| **제일 인기 있는** | **메뉴가** | **뭐예요?** |
| the most popular | dish | What is |

**Do you have any vegan recommendations?**
제일 인기 있는 ~이/가 뭐예요?

### 5 Key Sentences

- **제일 인기 있는 메뉴가 뭐예요?**
  [인끼인는]
  What is your most popular dish?

- **제일 인기 있는 게 뭐예요?**
  What is the most popular dish here?

- **제일 인기 있는 샐러드가 뭐예요?**
  What is your most popular salad?

- **가장 인기 있는 치킨이 뭐예요?**
  Which type of chicken dish is the most popular here?

- **가장 인기 있는 빵이 뭐예요?**
  What is your most popular bread?

**Speak like a native with natural expressions**

**I'm ready to order.**

**주문할게요.** 🔊
[주무날께요]

- Most times, '저기요', meaning 'over here', or '저기요, 주문할게요' are used.

**What are the specialties?**

**여기에서 뭐가 제일 잘 나가요?** 🔊

▶ **맛있어요** Delicious

**Then, I'll have one of those.**

**그럼, 그거 하나 주세요.** 🔊

**I'd like to have the regular flavour, please.**

**보통맛으로 주세요.** 🔊

▶ **순한맛** mild taste
▶ **매콤한 맛** a bit spicy taste
▶ **매운맛** spicy taste

- These days, more and more places have spicy options available for customers to choose. By checking the number of chilies next to a dish on the menu, you can tell which options are spicier.

**I'd like some more cheese, please.**

**치즈 추가해 주세요.** 🔊

▶ **라면사리** extra ramen noodles
▶ **떡** rice cake

**Can I have the sauce served separately, please?**

**소스는 따로 주세요.** 🔊
[쏘스]

- When eating Sweet and Sour Pork(탕수육), people who like their sauce as a dip instead of poured over, would request this way. It has become such a commonplace question that guests on variety shows are sometimes asked if they are 부먹파 (people who like their sauce poured over) or 찍먹파 (people who like their sauce as a dip). Isn't that such an easy way to find out about people's preferences and see if you'll become friends? Personally, I am a 찍먹파[찡먹파]!

**Is it enough for two people?**　　둘이 먹기에 양이 적당한가요? ◀》
　　　　　　　　　　　　　　　　　　[적땅항가요]

> **적당하다** Not too much and not too little - just right.

**Is it spicier than Shin Ramen?**　신라면보다 매운가요? ◀》
　　　　　　　　　　　　　　　　　[신나면]

● In Korea, Shin Ramen is the standard measure for spiciness level. Try Shin Ramen for yourself, and decide if it's too spicy or just okay for you. Then, when you see a dish on the menu that has 'hot' next to it, just ask the server this question.

**I'll order a little later.**　　조금 있다가 주문할게요. ◀》

● If you haven't decided what you want but the server has come to you, reply this way.

**What flavour would you like?**　무슨 맛으로 드릴까요? ◀》

Write down the appropriate sentence in the blank space and practice your pronunciations by reading out loud.

---

**Siwoo** _____? ❶

What is the most popular dish here?

**Employee** 로제 떡볶이가 제일 잘 나가요.

Rose Tteokbokki is the best.

**Siwoo** _____. ❷ 매콤한 맛은 많이 맵나요?

Then, I'll have one of those. Is the 매콤한 맛 very spicy?

**Employee** 네, 신라면보다 조금 더 매워요.

Yes, it's a little spicier than Shin Ramen.

**Siwoo** _____. ❸

Then I'll have the regular flavor.

**Employee** 네, 알겠습니다.

Sure.

---

**29**

TRACK 11

# 내일 저녁 7시에 예약할 수 있을까요?

**Can I make a reservation for tomorrow at 7 pm?**

 **Do you want to know** How to make a reservation at a restaurant?

Honestly speaking, making reservations is not common in Korean restaurants, However, it is common to make reservations for group diners. Or on special days, in order to eat special food at special places, you would also need to make a reservation individually. So, in order to do that, you need to mention "[your desired time] +에 예약할 수 있을까요?"

## Today's Pattern

| day/date+아침/점심/저녁 | time+에 | 예약할 수 있을까요? |
|---|---|---|
| **내일 저녁** | **7시에** | **예약할 수 있을까요?** |
| tomorrow evening | at 7 | Can I make a reservation? |

**Can I make a reservation for tomorrow at 7 pm?**
**~에 예약할 수 있을까요?**

## 5 Key Sentences

- **내일 저녁 7시에 예약할 수 있을까요?**
  [예야칼쑤이쓸까요]
  Can I make a reservation for tomorrow at 7 pm?

- **오늘 오후 2시에 예약할 수 있을까요?**
  Can I make a reservation for 2 p.m. today, please?

- **금요일 저녁 7시에 예약할 수 있을까요?**
  Can I make a reservation for Friday at 7 p.m., please?

- **내일 아침 8시에 예약할 수 있을까요?**
  Can I make a reservation for tomorrow at 8 a.m., please?

- **토요일 오전 11시에 예약할 수 있을까요?**
  Can I make a reservation for 11 a.m. on Saturday, please?

| | |
|---|---|
| **There are two people.** | 두 명이에요. 🔊 |

▸ **세 명** three people
▸ **네 명** four people

**Two adults and two children.** 어른 두 명에 아이 두 명이에요. 🔊

● 성인=어른 adult

**Can I make a reservation for a table by the window?** 창가쪽 자리로 예약할 수 있을까요? 🔊

▸ **안쪽** indoor seating

**I'd like to make a reservation for a (private) room.** 룸으로 예약하고 싶어요. 🔊

▸ **조용한 자리로** quict seating

**Can you prepare a baby chair?** 유아용 의자를 준비해 주실 수 있나요? 🔊

**How long do I have to wait?** 대기 시간이 얼마나 걸려요? 🔊

**Please put me on the waiting list.** 대기자 명단에 올려 주세요. 🔊

**I'll wait for a seat** 기다릴게요. 🔊

**It's okay. I'll come back next time.**

**괜찮아요. 다음에 올게요.** 🔊
- Say this if the waiting time is too long and you don't wan't to wait.

**Can I cancel my reservation?**

**예약을 취소할 수 있을까요?** 🔊

Write down the appropriate sentence in the blank space and practice your pronunciations by reading out loud.

---

**Minjun**
_____? ❶
Can I make a reservation for tomorrow at 7 pm?

**Employee** **네, 가능합니다. 몇 분이세요?**
Sure, it's possible. How many people are there?

**Minjun**
_____. ❷
It's for two people.

**Employee** **네, 전화하신 분 성함이 어떻게 되세요?**
Alright, may I have your name for the reservation?

**Minjun**
_____ ❸
It's Seo Minjun.

**Employee** **네, 서민준 님으로 예약해 드렸습니다.**
Okay, I made a reservation for Seo Hyun Sil.

---

**Answer**

❶ Can I make a reservation for tomorrow at 7 pm, please?
내일 저녁 7시에 예약할 수 있을까요?

❷ It's for two people.   두 명이에요.

❸ It's Seo Hyun Sil.   서민준입니다.

TRACK 13

# 여보세요, 배달 주문하려고 하는데요.

## Hello, I'd like to place an order for delivery.

 **Do you want to know How to order for a food delivery?**

Food delivery culture in Korea is so developed that Korea can be called 'Delivery Heaven.' Nowadays, Koreans usually use apps to order delivery. To order via the app, you need to register your credit card and verify your identity using your phone. However, it can be difficult for foreigners to use them because of the lengthy identification process required. So today, I will tell you how to order delivery by phone. First, dial the number and then say this: **"여보세요, 배달 주문하려고 하는데요."**

### Today's Pattern

| 여보세요, | N | 하려고 하는데요. |
|---|---|---|
| **여보세요,** | **배달 주문** | **하려고 하는데요.** |
| **Hello,** | **a food delivery order** | **I'd like to** |

**Hello, I'd like to place an order for delivery.**
**여보세요, ~주문하려고 하는데요.**

### 5 Key Sentences

- **여보세요, 배달 주문하려고 하는데요.**  Hello, I'd like to place an order for delivery.

- **여보세요, 치즈피자 하나 주문하려고 하는데요.**  Hello, I'd like to order one cheese pizza.

- **여보세요, 엽기 떡볶이 하나 주문하려고 하는데요.**  Hello, I'd like to order one yupgi tteokbokki.

- **여보세요, 찜닭 한 마리 주문하려고 하는데요.**  Hello, I'd like to order one braised
  [찜따칸마리]  chicken.

- **여보세요, 포장 주문하려고 하는데요.**  Hello, I'd like to order a pick-up.
  [주무나려고]

**Speak like a native with natural expressions**

---

**One fried chicken, please.**

프라이드치킨 한 마리 주세요. 🔊

▸ **짜장면 두 그릇** two bowls of
jjajangmyeon
▸ **불고기피자 한 판** one bulgogi pizza

---

**I'd like a boneless one,
please.**

뼈 없는 걸로 주세요. 🔊

▸ **순살로** Boneless (meat)

● 뼈 bone
● 뼈 없는 치킨 = 순살 치킨

---

**The address is 54 Hankuk-
ro 34beon-gil, and Alpha
Apartment 101dong 302.**

주소는 한국로34번길 54이구요,
알파 아파트 101동 302호요. 🔊

● Addresses in Korea are written in the
order <00로 00번길 00>. 00로 is the name
of the street, while 00번길 is the number
of the street. The last number refers to the
building's unique number. After this comes
the building name and apartment number.
Usually, apartments are written as 00동
00호, while buildings are written as 00층
00호.

---

**This is Yeouido Hangang Park,
please come to
Delivery Zone 2.**

여의도 한강공원이구요,
배달존 2로 와 주세요. 🔊

● When ordering delivery at the Han River,
you have to go to a delivery zone to receive
your order. There are three Han River
delivery zones, and you can look them up
on Naver maps.

---

**I'll pay by credit card.**

결제는 카드로 할게요. 🔊

▸ **현금으로** by cash

**35**

**How long will it take?**　　　얼마나 걸릴까요? 🔊

**Please call me when you get here.**　　　도착하면 전화 주세요. 🔊
[도차카면]

**Then, I'll order next time.**　　　그럼, 다음에 주문할게요. 🔊

● If the given waiting time is too long and you want to cancel your order, use this sentence.

**Hello, I ordered it an hour ago.**　　　여보세요, <u>1시간</u> 전에 주문한 사람인데요. 🔊

▸ **30분**

● If your delivery time has passed but your order still hasn't arrived, you can call again and use this sentence.

**I haven't got it yet.**　　　<u>아직도 배달이 안 와서요.</u> 🔊

▸ **음식이 잘못 와서** because the food is wrong
▸ **국물이 다 새서** because the soup
　[궁무리]　　　　　leaked

● You can use this sentence when making a complaint.

Write down the appropriate sentence in the blank space and practice your pronunciations by reading out loud.

**Sooah** _____. ❶

Hello, I'd like to order one fried chicken.

**Employee** 네, 프라이드 한 마리요. 주소 불러 주시겠어요?

Alright, one fried chicken. May I have your address, please?

**Sooah** _____. ❷

It's 54 Hankuk-ro 34beon-gil, and Alpha Apartment 101dong 302.

**Employee** 네, 알파아파트 101동 302호, 맞으시죠?

Okay, Alpha Apartment 101dong 302ho, right?

**Sooah** 네, _____? ❸

Yes. How long will it take?

**Employee** 지금 주문이 밀려서 한 40분 정도 걸립니다.

It takes about 40 minutes because I'm behind on my order.

### Answer

❶ Hello, I'd like to order one fried chicken.
여보세요, 프라이드치킨 한 마리 주문하려고 하는데요.

❷ The address is 54 Hankuk-ro 34beon-gil, and Alpha Apartment 101dong 302. 한국로34번길 54, 알파 아파트 101동 302호요.

❸ How long will it take? 얼마나 걸릴까요?

# UNIT 2

# Shopping

# 이거 얼마예요?
How much is this?

 **Do you want to know How to ask the price of an item?**

When you are curious about the price of an item you like, you can ask this way: '이거 얼마예요?' How much is this? Because '이거' means 'this', you can also replace it with the name of the item you are asking about. For example, '이 가방' (this bag) or '이 양말' (these socks). Simple, isn't it?

### Today's Pattern

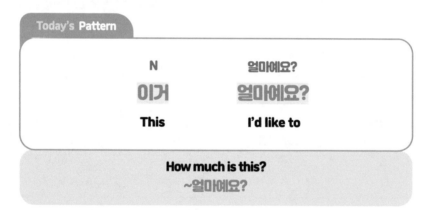

| N | 얼마예요? |
|---|---|
| **이거** | **얼마예요?** |
| **This** | **I'd like to** |

**How much is this?**
~얼마예요?

### 5 Key Sentences

- **이거 얼마예요?**     How much is this?
- **이 티셔츠 얼마예요?**     How much is this t-shirt?
- **이 호떡 하나 얼마예요?**     How much for one hotteok?
  [호떠카나]
- **이 계란 한 판 얼마예요?**     How much is a tray of eggs?
- **이 사과 한 봉지에 얼마예요?**     How much is a bag of apples?

**Speak like a native with natural expressions**

| | |
|---|---|
| **How much is that (item) over there?** | 저기 있는 건 얼마예요? ◁<br>[인능건] |

**Can I get a discount if I buy a lot?**

많이 사면 할인되나요? ◁

▶ **2개 사면** if I buy two
▶ **세트로 사면** if I buy a set

● If you state the conditions for a discount first, use the connector '면/으면', which is similar to the 'if' clause in English.

**Can you give me a little more discount?**

좀 더 깎아 주실 수 있나요? ◁
[까까주실쑤인나요]

● 깎다 to haggle
● 가격을 깎다 give a discount

**What's the price of this Hotteok?**

이 호떡 어떻게 팔아요? ◁

● When shopping at street stalls, it can be hard to tell what price the items are sold for, and how many are sold. At such times, you can ask like this, and you may receive an answer like '1개에 2000원' (one for 2000 won).

**How much is this coffee table after 20% discount?**

이 테이블은 20% 할인하면 얼마예요? ◁
[이십프로]
or [이십퍼센트]

**Is it cheaper if I buy this skincare in a set?**

스킨케어는 세트로 사면 더 저렴한가요? ◁
[저려만가요]

**Is there an additional charge if I change it to soy milk?**

두유로 바꾸면 추가 요금이 있나요? ◁

**Is the price on this tag discounted?**

이 택에 있는 가격은 할인된 금액인가요? 🔊

[이 태게 인는 가겨근 하린된 그매긴가요]

**How much more do I need to pay?**

제가 얼마 더 드리면 돼요? 🔊

**What is the additional charge for upgrading to a deluxe room?**

디럭스 룸으로 업그레이드하면 추가 요금이 얼마예요? 🔊

Write down the appropriate sentence in the blank space and practice your pronunciations by reading out loud.

When you go to a traditional market, merchants often speak informally to customers. People who speak informally are usually older people. In Korea, there has been a custom of older people speaking informally to younger people for quite a long time. I prepared a casual conversation so that you don't get surprised even if you hear it informally, so let's practice natural conversations.

Siwoo | _____ ? ❶
How much are these peaches?

**Merchant** | **한 상자에 9000원.**
9,000 won per box.

Siwoo | **그럼,** _____ ? ❷
Then, what about this watermelon?

**Merchant** | **18000원.**
18000 won.

Siwoo | **사장님, 제가 10개씩 사면** _____ ? ❸
Sir, can you give me a discount if I buy 10 each?

**Merchant** | **10개씩? 음… 그래, 깎아 줘야지 뭐.**
10 each? Well…okay, I'll give you a discount.

**Answer**

❶ How much are these peaches? 이 복숭아는 얼마예요?
❷ What about this watermelon? 이 수박은요?
❸ Can you give me a discount? 좀 깎아 주실 수 있나요?

# 이거 입어 볼 수 있을까요?
## Can I try this on?

TRACK 17

 **Do you want to know How to ask to try on clothes?**

When you visit Korea, do you find yourself wanting to buy all the pretty clothes? Well, today, let's look at some expressions that are often used when shopping for clothes. And let's find out the expressions you can use especially when you want to try on clothes.

---

**Today's Pattern**

| N | 입어 볼 수 있을까요? |
|---|---|
| **이거** | **입어 볼 수 있을까요?** |
| This | Can I try ~ on? |

**Can I try this on?**
**~입어 볼 수 있을까요?**

---

**5 Key Sentences**

- **이거 입어 볼 수 있을까요?**　　　　Can I try this on?
  [이버볼쑤이쓸까여]

- **이 원피스 입어 볼 수 있을까요?**　　Can I try on this dress?

- **이 바지 입어 볼 수 있을까요?**　　　Can I try these pants on?

- **이 티셔츠 입어 볼 수 있을까요?**　　Can I try on this t-shirt?

- **이 치마 입어 볼 수 있을까요?**　　　Can I try on this skirt?

**Speak like a native with natural expressions**

**I'll take this one.**

이걸로 살게요. 🔊

▸ **주세요** (please) give me

**Where is the fitting room?**

피팅룸이 어디예요? 🔊

▸ **탈의실**
● '피팅룸' and '탈의실' both mean fitting room.

**Do you have this in any other color?**

다른 색상은 없어요? 🔊

▸ **색깔** color

**Do you have this dress in XL size?**

이 원피스 XL사이즈도 있나요? 🔊
[엑스라지]

● Women's sizes in Korea are 55 (read as 오오), 66 (육육), 77(칠칠), and 88(팔팔), which are small, medium, large and extra-large respectively.
● Men's sizes are 90, 95, 100 and 105, corresponding to small, medium, large and extra-large.

**Do you have these leggings in navy colour?**

이 레깅스 남색은 없나요? 🔊

**What floor is the children's clothing section on?**

아동복은 몇 층에 있어요? 🔊

▸ **남성복** men's clothing
▸ **여성복** women's clothing

**45**

**I'm looking for a short-sleeved T-shirt.**

반팔 티셔츠를 찾고 있는데요. 🔊

▷ **긴팔 티셔츠** long-sleeved t-shirt
▷ **반바지** shorts
▷ **긴바지** pants

**Is there a tie that goes well with this shirt?**

이 셔츠랑 잘 어울리는 넥타이가 있을까요? 🔊

▷ **치마**
▷ **블라우스**

**Do you have swimsuits for girls under 5 years old?**

5살 아래 여자 아이 수영복도 있나요? 🔊

▷ **5살쯤 되는** around 5 years

**Can I see the coat displayed in the shopwindows?**

저 쇼윈도에 걸린 코트 좀 볼 수 있을까요? 🔊

▷ **재킷** Jacket
▷ **가디건** Cardigan

Write down the appropriate sentence in the blank space and practice your pronunciations by reading out loud.

Seohyeon _____ ? ❶

Do you have this dress in XL size?

**Employee** 네, 여기 있어요.

Yes, here it is.

Seohyeon _____ ? ❷

Can I try it on?

**Employee** 네, 가능하세요.

Sure, you can.

Seohyeon _____ ? ❸

Where is the fitting room?

**Employee** 저 오른쪽에 있어요.

It's over there on the right.

**Answer**

❶ Do you have this dress in XL size? 이 원피스 XL사이즈도 있나요?

❷ Can I try it on? 입어 볼 수 있을까요?

❸ Where is the fitting room? 피팅룸이 어디예요?

**47**

TRACK 19

# 지성 피부에 어떤 스킨이 좋아요?
## What kind of toner is good for oily skin?

 **Do you want to know How to shop for cosmetics?**

Korea is famous for being the go-to place to buy high quality yet inexpensive cosmetics. When in Korea, be sure to visit large cosmetic shops like Olive Young and Lalavla. In most stores, you can try on the products; so even if it is a brand that is new to you, you can safely check on the quality by yourself. Also, before going, practice how to say your skin type: oily (지성), dry (건성) or sensitive (민감성). It will be useful when asking the store clerk to recommend good products for you.

## Today's **Pattern**

| Adj+피부에 | 어떤 N+이/가 | 좋아요? |
|---|---|---|
| **지성 피부에** | **어떤 스킨이** | **좋아요?** |
| for oily skin | What kind of toner | is good |

**What kind of toner is good for oily skin?**
~피부에 어떤 ~이/가 좋아요?

## 5 Key Sentences

- **지성 피부에 어떤 스킨이 좋아요?**　　What kind of skin is good for oily skin?
- **건성 피부에 어떤 쿠션이 좋아요?**　　Which cushion is good for dry skin?
- **건성 피부에 어떤 에센스가 좋아요?**　　What kind of essence is good for dry skin?
- **민감성 피부에 어떤 마스크팩이 좋아요?**　　Which mask pack is good for sensitive skin?
- **지성 피부에 어떤 파운데이션이 좋아요?**　　What kind of foundation is suitable for oily skin?

**Speak like a native with natural expressions**

**Please recommend a face powder for oily skin.**

지성 피부용 파우더 추천해 주세요. 🔊

▸ **건성 피부** dry skin

● The '용' here means 'purpose'. So '지성 피부용' is an abbreviated way to say 'dedicated for use on oily skin'.

**Please suggest a blusher for tanned skin.**

태닝 피부에 어울리는 블러셔 좀 추천해 주세요. 🔊
[추처내]

**I'm looking for a matte lipstick.**

매트한 립스틱을 찾고 있어요. 🔊

▸ **촉촉한** moist

**I'm looking for a natural-coloured eye shadow.**

자연스러운 색상의 아이섀도를 찾고 있어요. 🔊

▸ **화려한** vibrant, colourful

**Which cushion has the best coverage?**

커버력이 제일 좋은 쿠션은 뭐예요? 🔊

▸ **지속성** long-lasting

**Is it for removing blackheads?**

블랙헤드 제거용 제품인가요? 🔊

▸ **여드름** acne
▸ **기미** freckles
▸ **주름** wrinkles

**I like the scent.**

향이 마음에 들어요. 🔊

▸ **은은하네요** delicate
▸ **너무 강하네요** too strong

**49**

**Can I apply this essence after skin toner?**

이 에센스는 스킨 다음에 바르면 되나요? ◁

▷ **언제** when

● 바르다 means 'to apply'.

**Will this concealer cover my pimples?**

이 컨실러로 제 여드름이 커버될까요? ◁

▷ **주근깨가** freckles
▷ **상처가** scars

**Please recommend a lip gloss that goes well with a warm skin tone.**

웜톤에 어울리는 립글로즈 추천해 주세요. ◁

▷ **쿨톤** cool tone

● Do you know your personal colour? If gold suits you better and your face has yellow tones, then you are warm toned. If silver jewelry suits you better and your face has pink tones, then you are cool toned. If you let the store clerk know your personal color, they will be able to give you better recommendations.

Write down the appropriate sentence in the blank space and practice your pronunciations by reading out loud.

**Sooah** _____ ? ❶

What kind of skin toner is good for dry skin?

**Employee** 알파이즘에서 나온 이 스킨이 잘 맞으실 거예요.

This skin toner from Alphaism will suit you well.

**Sooah** 그래요? _____ ? ❷

Really? I like the scent.

**Employee** 은은한 향기 좋아하시나 봐요.
그럼 이 에센스도 한번 발라 드릴게요. 요즘 진짜 잘 나가요.

I guess you like soft scents. Then I'll apply this essence on you
too. It's really popular these days.

**Sooah** _____ ? ❸

When should I apply this essence?

**Employee** 스킨 바르고 난 다음에 바르시면 돼요.

You can put it on after applying toner.

---

**Answer**

❶ What kind of skin lotion is good for dry skin?    건성 피부에 어떤 스킨이 좋아요?
❷ I like the scent.    향기가 마음에 들어요.
❸ When should I apply this essence?    이 에센스는 언제 바르면 되나요?

**51**

TRACK 21

# 신발이 좀 큰 거 같아요.
## I think these shoes are a bit big.

 **Do you want to know Expressions you need when buying shoes?**

In this lesson, let's study some expressions used when shopping for shoes. First, you have to check your shoe size because sizes in South Korea are different. Korean shoe sizes are measured in millimeters, such as 230mm and 235mm. If you plan to buy shoes in Korea, do not forget to find out what your size is.

---

**Today's Pattern**

| 신발이 | 좀+adj | 거 같아요. |
|---|---|---|
| **신발이** | **좀 큰** | **거 같아요.** |
| these shoes | a bit big | I think ~is/are |

**I think these shoes are a bit big.**
신발이 좀 ~ㄴ 거 같아요.

---

**5 Key Sentences**

- **신발이 좀 큰 거 같아요.**  I think these shoes are a bit big.
- **신발이 좀 작은 거 같아요.**  I think these shoes are a bit small.
- **신발이 좀 헐렁한 거 같아요.**  I think these shoes are a bit loose.
- **신발이 좀 끼는 거 같아요.**  I think my shoes are getting stuck.
- **신발이 좀 불편한 것 같아요.**  I think my shoes are a little uncomfortable.
  [불펴난걷가타요]

**Speak like a native with natural expressions**

**Do you have dress shoes for men?**

<u>남성용</u> 가죽 구두 있나요? 🔊
[인나요]

▸ **여성용** for women

**I would like to look at some heels.**

<u>하이힐</u> 좀 보려고요. 🔊

▸ **런닝화** running shoes
▸ **스니커즈** sneakers

● If the store personnel asks what you came in for by saying '찾으시는 거 있으세요?', answer using the following pattern: what you want to buy + 좀 보려고요.

**Do you have any cheaper sandals?**

좀 더 <u>저렴한</u> 샌들은 없나요? 🔊
[저려만]

▸ **부츠** Boots
▸ **슬리퍼** Slippers

**Can I see some shoes for the beach?**

<u>해변에서</u> 신을 만한 신발 좀 볼 수 있을까요? 🔊
[시늘마난]

▸ **평소에 편하게** always comfortable

**I will just look around**

그냥 구경 좀 할게요. 🔊

▸ **하려고요**

● 할게요=하려고요

● You can say this when you don't have anything you really want to buy but you want to look around the shop.

**Can I try these on?**

이걸로 신어 볼 수 있을까요? 🔊
[시너볼쑤]

**These fit me perfectly.**

이게 딱 맞아요. 🔊
[딱 마자요]

**Do you have one size smaller than these?**

이것보다 한 사이즈 작은 거 있나요? 🔊

▶ 큰 거 one size up

**Do you have these in a different colour?**

같은 걸로 다른 색은 없나요? 🔊

▶ 검정색 black (colour)
▶ 골드 gold (colour)

● Use this to ask when you like something but would like to know if it is available in a different color.

**Do you have these in size 250?**

이걸로 250 사이즈 있나요? 🔊
[이백오십]

▶ 더 른 bigger
▶ 더 작은 smaller

## Reference

● **Women's shoe sizes**
American sizes: 5 5.5 6 6.5 7 7.5 8 8.5 9 9.5 10 10.5
Korean sizes: 220 225 230 235 240 245 250 255 260 265 270 275

● **Men's shoe sizes**
American sizes: 3 3.5 4 4.5 5 5.5 6 6.5 7 7.5 8 8.5 9 9.5 10 10.5 11 11.5 12 12.5
Korean sizes(mm): 205 210 215 220 225 230 235
240 245 250 255 260 265 270 275 280 285 290 295 300

Write down the appropriate sentence in the blank space and practice your pronunciations by reading out loud.

**Employee**　　찾으시는 거 있으세요?

Is there anything you are looking for?

**Minjun**　　네, _____. ❶

Yes, I'd like to see some sandals.

**Employee**　　요즘 이게 잘 나가요. 사이즈가 어떻게 되세요?

These sandals are popular these days. What's your size?

**Minjun**　　**280이요.** (After trying on the shoes) _____. ❷

280mm. (After trying on the shoes) I think my shoes are a bit too big.

**Employee**　　그럼 한 사이즈 더 작은 걸로 드릴게요. 이제 어떠세요?

Then I'll give you a smaller size. How did it feel?

**Minjun**　　(After changing shoes) _____. ❸

(After changing shoes) This fits perfectly.

---

**Answer**

❶ I'd like to see some sandals.　　샌들 좀 보려고요.
❷ I think my shoes are a bit too big.　　신발이 좀 큰 거 같아요.
❸ This fits perfectly.　　이게 딱 맞아요.

TRACK 23

# 쇼핑 카트는 어디에 있어요?
**Where can I find a shopping cart?**

 **Do you know how to get around the grocery store?**

Today, we will take a look at expressions you can use at the grocery store. First, 'grocery store' in Korean is '마트' (like the English word 'mart'). Most 마트 are very wide, and there will be many times when you have to ask for the location of an item. At such times, you can ask, "(the section or item you want)+은/는 어디에 있어요?".

## Today's **Pattern**

| N+은/는 | 어디에 있어요? |
|---|---|
| **쇼핑 카트는** | **어디에 있어요?** |
| **a shopping cart** | **Where can I find** |

**Where can I find a shopping cart?**
**~은/는 어디에 있어요?**

## 5 Key Sentences

- **쇼핑 카트는 어디에 있어요?**　　Where can I find a shopping cart?
- **유제품은 어디에 있어요?**　　Where can I find the dairy products?
- **육류는 어디에 있어요?**　　Where can I find the meat (section)?
  [융뉴]
- **계산대는 어디에 있어요?**　　Where is the checkout counter?
- **밀키트는 어디에 있어요?**　　Where can I find the meal kit?

- A meal kit(밀키트) in Korean means a package that includes pre-portioned ingredients and seasoning, a recipe. It's not a subscription service so people can get it from supermarkets or online shopping malls. Nowadays Korea's meal kit trend is increasing sharply.

**Speak like a native with natural expressions** 🎧

---

**I ran out of eggs.**

계란이 떨어졌어요. 🔊

[떠러져써요]

▸ **사과가** apples
▸ **식빵이** sliced bread

---

**Do you have cilantro?**

고수 있나요? 🔊

● You can use this expression to check if the product you want is being sold at the store.

---

**I can't find the whipped cream.** 휘핑크림을 못 찾겠어요. 🔊

---

**I'm grocery shopping.**

장 보고 있어요. 🔊

● 장을 보다 to do grocery shopping

---

**Please take this out.**

이건 빼 주세요. 🔊

● You can use this expression when you want to exclude something before you pay.

---

**Can I use my coupon?**

쿠폰 사용할 수 있나요? 🔊

→**포인트** points

---

**Can I get a discount on this too?**

이것도 할인되나요? 🔊

● At marts, there are often discount events such as buy-one-get-one free deals (known as one plus one) or buy four items for 10000 won (about $8). Use this expression to check if something you want is on sale.

**I brought my shopping basket.**

**장바구니 가져왔어요.** ◁»
[장빠구니]

- At the counter, the staff often asks if you need a bag by saying '봉투 필요하세요?'. If you brought your own bag, you can respond using this.

**I'd like a paper bag, please.**

**종이백 하나 주세요.** ◁»
[종이빽]

▷ **비닐 봉투** plastic bag
▷ **종량제 봉투** a standard plastic garbage bag

- In Korea, each city, county or autonomous province has their own, which can be used when throwing out the trash. These bags can be purchased at supermarkets or convenience stores.

**Do you want to save points?**

**포인트 적립해 드릴까요?** ◁»
[정니패드릴까요]

- The cashier will usually ask this right before calculating your bill. If you have a membership, then you can reply '네', and give your phone number checking for your membership. If not, just say '아니요'.

Write down the appropriate sentence in the blank space and practice your pronunciations by reading out loud.

Sooah  **저기요,** _____. ❶

Excuse me, I can't find the whipped cream.

Employee  **아, 오른쪽으로 쭉 가시면 32번 유제품 코너에 있습니다.**

Oh, if you go straight to the right, it's in the dairy section 32.

Sooah  **네, 거기** _____? ❷

I see, do you have cheese there?

Employee  **네, 그것도 유제품 코너에 있을 거예요.**

Yes, that should be in the dairy section, too.

Sooah  (유제품 코너에서) _____? ❸

(in the dairy section) Is this ricotta cheese on a buy-one-get-one-free sale?

Employee  **네, 다른 치즈랑 같이 사시면 할인 적용됩니다.**

Sure, you can get a discount if you buy it with other cheese.

**Answer**

❶ I can't find the whipped cream. 휘핑크림을 못 찾겠어요.

❷ Do you have cheese there? 거기 치즈도 있나요?

❸ Is this ricotta cheese on a buy-one-get-one-free sale?
이 리코타 치즈도 1+1 할인되나요?

TRACK 25

# 한국 소설 코너는 어디에 있어요?
## Where is the Korean novel section?

 **Do you want to know How to find books at the bookstore?**

Do you like books? If you do, then you will surely enjoy going to popular book-stores and shopping for books that you can only buy in Korea. In Korea, the largest bookstore is Kyobo Book Center (교보문고), which is my personal favourite. The most popular bookstore among tourists are the hip and cool stores like Arc n Book and Book Park. Be sure to find and visit a bookstore you like while in Korea.

---

**Today's Pattern**

| N | 코너는 | 어디에 있어요? |
|---|---|---|
| **한국 소설** | **코너는** | **어디에 있어요?** |
| the Korean novel | section | Where is |

**Where is the Korean novel section?**
~코너는 어디에 있어요?

---

**5 Key  Sentences**

- **한국 소설 코너는 어디에 있어요?**　　Where is the Korean novel section?
  [항국]
- **베스트셀러 코너는 어디에 있어요?**　　Where is the bestsellers section?
- **만화책 코너는 어디에 있어요?**　　Where is the comic book section?
  [마놔책/마나책]
- **요리책 코너는 어디에 있어요?**　　Where is the cookbook section?
- **수필 코너는 어디에 있어요?**　　Where is the essay collections section?

## Speak like a native with natural expressions

**Where is the section for novels by the author named Chung Serang?**

**정세랑 작가의 소설은 어디에 있어요?** 🔊

▷ 김연수 작가의 수필

● I would like to introduce you to two of my favourite authors. They are Chung Serang and Kim Yeonsu. Those who want to read the original editions of Korean literature should give books by these authors a try. Essay collections might be easier to read than novels. Kim Yeonsu's essays are really good.

**I don't know the title of the book.**

**책 제목은 잘 모르겠어요.** 🔊

▷ **작가는** the writer
[작까는]

▷ **출판사는** the publisher
▷ **출판연도는** the year of publication

**Excuse me, can you help me find a book?**

**저기요, 책 찾는 것 좀 도와주시겠어요?** 🔊

▷ **실례합니다** Excuse me

**I know the writer's name.**

**작가 이름은 알아요.** 🔊

▷ **책 제목** the book title

**Are there any translations from other publishers?**

**다른 출판사에서 번역된 건 없나요?** 🔊

● Have you ever wanted to read an English novel in Korean? If you have any favorite English books, try reading them in Korean too. It makes it easier to read novels that have movie adaptations you have watched previously, as you already know the contents.

**Please recommend a book for beginners in Korean.**

한국어 초보자한테 어떤 책이 좋을지 추천해 주세요. ◁»

▷ **6살 아이에게** for a 6-year old

**Who is the best novelist these days?**

요즘 제일 잘 나가는 소설가는 누구예요? ◁»

▷ **로맨스 소설이 뭐예요?** What is the most popular romance novel these days?
▷ **자기계발서가 뭐예요?** What is the most popular self-help book these days?

**This book is out of print.**

이 책은 절판됐어요. ◁»

▷ **이제 안 나와요** It is not released anymore

**Look it up in a secondhand bookstore.**

헌책방에서 찾아보세요. ◁»
[헌책빵]

▷ **인터넷 서점** Internet bookstore

● If you like second-hand bookstores, also check out Aladdin Used Books (알라딘 중고서점). It is a bookstore selling second-hand books that I really like.

**I'm sorry, but we're out of stock.**

죄송하지만 재고가 없네요. ◁»

▷ **재고** stock

Write down the appropriate sentence in the blank space and practice your pronunciations by reading out loud.

Mary _____? **❶**

Excuse me, can you help me find a book?

**Employee** 네, 어떤 책 찾으세요?

Sure, what book are you looking for?

Mary _____. **❷**

It's a novel by writer Chung Serang.

**Employee** 책 제목이 어떻게 돼요?

What's the title of the book?

Mary _____. **❸**

I don't know the title of the book.

**Employee** 그럼, G 문학 코너에서 찾아보세요.

Then, you can look it up in the G Literature section.

---

### Answer

❶ Excuse me, can you help me find a book?
저기요, 책 찾는 것 좀 도와주시겠어요?

❷ It's a novel by writer Chung Serang.  정세랑 작가의 소설이요.

❸ I don't know the title of the book.  책 제목은 잘 모르겠어요.

TRACK 27

# 카드로 할게요.
**I'll pay by card.**

 **Do you want to know** How to ask if they accept cash or credit?

If you want to check the accepted payment method, you can do so using a very simple sentence pattern. The pattern is "(payment method) + 되나요?". Here, the verb '되다' means 'it works' or 'it is okay'. By the way, most places in Korea take card payments. In fact, the number of places where cash payments are not accepted is increasing. The next pattern will be very helpful to you: '(payment method)~ 로/으로 할게요.'

---

**Today's Pattern**

| N+로/으로 | 할게요. |
|---|---|
| **카드로** | **할게요.** |
| **by card** | **I'll pay** |

**I'll pay by card.**
~로/으로 할게요.

---

**5 Key Sentences**

- **카드로 할게요.**　　　　　I'll pay by card.

- **현금으로 할게요.**　　　　Let me pay in cash.
  [현그므로]

- **일시불로 할게요.**　　　　I'd like to pay in full.

- **3개월 할부로 할게요.**　　I'll pay in three monthly installments.
  [삼개월]

- **6개월 할부로 할게요.**　　I'll make a six-month installment plan.

**Speak like a native with natural expressions**

**How would you like to make your payment?**

**어떻게 결제해 드릴까요?** 🔊
[어떠케]

- When paying by credit card, the staff will ask you this. They want to know if you would like to pay in installments or in full.

**Can I pay by credit card?**

**카드 결제 가능한가요?** 🔊

▸ **되나요?**

- When talking about payments, both '가능하다' and '되다' can be used interchangeably.

**It's on me this time.**

**이번엔 제가 살게요.** 🔊

▸ **저녁은** dinner
▸ **밥은** the meal

**It's on me today.**

**오늘은 제가 쏠게요.** 🔊

- '쏘다' is slang for the verb 'to buy' (사다). However, it is frequently used in everyday speech. Instead of being rude, it actually has a more 'fun' nuance to it. Therefore, it can be used in most situations except formal ones.

**I'm sorry, but this card does not work.**

**죄송하지만 이 카드는 결제가 안 되네요.** 🔊
[결쩨]

- Cashiers say this when the card payment does not work because the card limit has been reached or because there is a problem with the card.

**65**

**You can only pay by card here.**  이곳에서는 <u>카드 결제</u>만 가능합니다. ◁€

> **현금 결제** cash payment

- In Korea, Some stores only accept credit card payments.

**Would you like to pay in full or in installments?**  일시불로 해 드릴까요, 할부로 해 드릴까요? ◁€

**Would you like to pay in cash or a credit card?**  현금으로 하실 건가요,
[형그므로하실껑가요]

카드로 하실 건가요? ◁€
[하실껑가요]

**Can we pay separately?**  <u>따로따로</u> 결제되나요? ◁€

> **한 사람씩** each person

**Do you accept cash only?**  <u>현금만</u> <u>받으시나요</u>? ◁€

> **되나요**

- In this context, '받으시나요 and 되나요'? are used in the same sense.

Write down the appropriate sentence in the blank space and practice your pronunciations by reading out loud.

**Seohyeon**
(현금 내면서) **계산할게요.**
(Paying cash) I'll pay now.

**Employee**
**죄송하지만,** _____. ❶
I'm sorry, but we only accept credit cards.

**Seohyeon**
**그래요? 그럼 카드 드릴게요.**
Really? Then I'll give you my card.

**Employee**
_____ ? ❷
Would you like to pay in full or in installments?

**Seohyeon**
_____. ❸
I'd like to pay in full.

**Employee**
**네, 결제되셨습니다.**
Sure, your payment has been made.

**Answer**

❶ We only accept credit cards.   이 곳에서는 신용카드 결제만 가능합니다.
❷ Would you like to pay in full or in installments?
　　　　　　　　　　　　　　　일시불로 해 드릴까요, 할부로 해 드릴까요?
❸ I'd like to pay in full.　　일시불로 할게요.

TRACK 29

# 이거 교환하고 싶어요.
**I'd like to exchange this.**

 **Do you want to know How to ask for a refund or an exchange?**

After shopping, what would you do if you want an exchange (교환) or a refund (환불)? You first have to check if you have your receipt and read the refund/exchange rules on it. After checking for your eligibility for an exchange or refund, you can visit the store with the credit card you used to pay. At the counter, show the cashier the item you purchased, and then say, "안녕하세요, 이거 교환하고 싶어요."

---

**Today's Pattern**

V+하고 싶어요.

**이거**      **교환하고 싶어요.**

**This**      **I'd like to exchange**

**I'd like to exchange this.**
이거 ~고 싶어요.

---

**5 Key Sentences**

- **이거 교환하고 싶어요.**    I'd like to exchange this.
- **이거 사고 싶어요.**    I'd like to buy this
- **이거 먹고 싶어요.**    I want to eat this
  [먹꼬시퍼요]
- **이거 바꾸고 싶어요.**    I'd like to change this
- **이거 환불하고 싶어요.**    I'd like to get a refund for this
  [환부라고]

**Speak like a native with natural expressions**

| | |
|---|---|
| **What's the issue with this clothing item?** | 옷에 무슨 문제 있나요? |
| **It's too big for me.** | 저한테 너무 커요. |
| | ▸ **작아요** small |
| **It doesn't fit.** | 사이즈가 안 맞아요. |
| **There's a stain on it.** | 여기 얼룩이 있어요. |
| | ▸ **구멍** hole |
| **I didn't notice when I bought it.** | 살 때는 몰랐어요. |
| **Do you have the receipt with you?** | 영수증 가져오셨나요? |
| | ▸ **결제하신 카드** the card you paid with |
| **I lost my receipt.** | 영수증을 잃어버렸어요.<br>[이러버려써요] |
| **Can I exchange it?** | 교환할 수 있을까요?<br>[교와날쑤이쓸까요] |
| | ▸ **환불** refund |
| | ● This is less direct and softer than immediately saying "I want to exchange this" (교환하고 싶어요). |
| **I'd like to get a refund for this jacket.** | 이 재킷을 환불해 주세요.<br>[자케슬] |
| | ▸ **모자를** hat |
| | ▸ **신발을** shoes |

**69**

**I'm sorry, but you can't get a refund after 14 days.**

**죄송하지만 14일이 지나서 환불이 안 됩니다.** ◁  [십싸이리]

- The refund or exchange rules in most places are stated on the receipt. Make sure to check them before going to the store.

Write down the appropriate sentence in the blank space and practice your pronunciations by reading out loud.

**Sooah**  안녕하세요, _____. ❶

Hello, I'd like to refund this.

**Employee**  옷에 무슨 문제가 있나요?

Is there a problem with it?

**Sooah**  _____. ❷

It's too big for me.

**Employee**  _____? ❸

Do you have your receipt?

**Sooah**  네, 여기 있어요.

Yes, here you go.

**Employee**  죄송하지만 이 제품은 할인 상품이라 환불이 안 됩니다.

I'm sorry, but this product is on sale, so you can't get a refund.

**Answer**

❶ I'd like a refund on this.   이거 환불하고 싶어요.
❷ It's too big for me.   저한테 너무 커요.
❸ Do you have your receipt?   영수증 가지고 오셨나요?

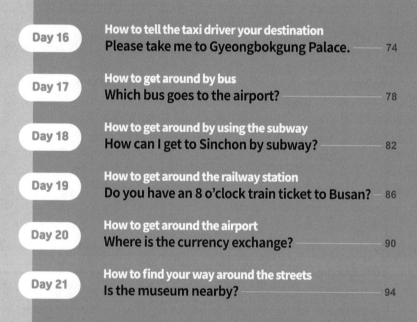

**UNIT 3**

# Transport & Directions

TRACK 31

# 경복궁으로 가 주세요.
## Please take me to Gyeongbokgung Palace.

 **Do you want to know How to tell the taxi driver your destination?**

In Korean, 'taxi driver' is '택시 기사' and when speaking to them, we say '기사님'. When you want to tell the 택시 기사 your destination, you need to say, "(Destination) +로 가 주세요." This means "Please go to (destination)". When you are close to your destination and want them to stop, you can simply say "(Destination)+에서 세 워주세요"

### Today's Pattern

| N+로/으로 | 가 주세요. |
|:---:|:---:|
| **경복궁으로** | **가 주세요.** |
| to Gyeongbokgung Palace. | Please take me |

**Please take me to Gyeongbokgung Palace.**
~로/으로 가 주세요.

### 5 Key Sentences

- **경복궁으로 가 주세요.**　　　Please take me to Gyeongbokgung Palace.
- **강남역으로 가 주세요.**　　　Please go to Gangnam station.
  [강남녁]
- **북촌 한옥마을로 가 주세요.**　Please take me to Bukcheon Hanok Village.
- **홍대로 가 주세요.**　　　　　Please go to Hongdae.
- **코엑스로 가 주세요.**　　　　Please take me to Coex.

74

**Speak like a native with natural expressions** 🎧

**Please pull over here.**

이 앞에서 세워 주세요. 🔊

**Please go to Alpha Cafe at 23 Itaewon-ro 1-gil, Yongsan-gu.**

용산구 이태원로 1길 23번지 알파카페로 가 주세요. 🔊

- When giving your address to the taxi driver, omit the name of the city, and then list everything else in the following order: XX구, YY로, ZZ길, 00번지, name of destination

**Please let me off in front of Gwanghwamun Station.**

광화문 역 앞에서 내려 주세요. 🔊
[광와문녁]

▸ **광화문역 2번 출구** Gwanghwamun Station, 2nd exit

- If you are getting off at a subway station, by giving the exit number will ensure that you get off at a more accurate location.

**Could you please go faster?**

좀 빨리 가 주실 수 있으세요? 🔊

▸ **천천히** slowly

**How long does it take to get there?**

거기까지 대략 얼마나 걸려요? 🔊

**Sir, please open the trunk.**

기사님, 트렁크 좀 열어 주세요. 🔊

- Use this expression when you have a lot of luggage to stow.

**How much is the approximate fare to get there?**

거기까지 요금이 대략 얼마예요? 🔊

- As of 2022, the standard fare in medium-sized taxis is 3,800 won for up to 2 km, and 6,500 won for up to 3 km with deluxe taxis (based on Seoul prices).

**75**

**Can we go past Samcheong-dong Street on the way?**

가는 길에 <u>삼청동 거리</u>를 지나서 갈 수 있을까요? ◁⅋

▸ **해안로를** a coastal route
▸ **가로수길을** Garosu-gil

● Garosu-gil is a famous street located in Sinsa-dong, Gangnam. It is a tourist destination that many foreigners visit because there are many shops and alleys to see.

● Is there a place you want to pass by while driving to your destination? If so, use this pattern: "가는 길에 (where you want to pass by)을/를 지나서 갈 수 있을까요?"

**Is it far from here?**

여기에서 먼가요? ◁⅋

▸ **가까운** close

**Sir, I want a quiet taxi ride**

기사님, 조용히 가고 싶어요. ◁⅋
[조용이]

● Sometimes you might meet a taxi driver who doesn't drive quietly and keeps making unnecessary conversation. When you want to ask them to drive quietly, say this.

Write down the appropriate sentence in the blank space and practice your pronunciations by reading out loud.

**Taxi Driver**   **안녕하세요. 어디로 가세요?.**

Hello. Where to, ma'am?

**Seohyeon** _____? ❶

Please go to Lotte World. Is it far from here?

**Taxi Driver**   **멀다고 봐야죠. 한 1시간쯤 걸려요.**

It's far away. It takes about an hour.

**Seohyeon** _____? ❷ **제가 급해서요.**

Can you go faster, please? I'm in a hurry.

**Taxi Driver**   **그래요, 그럼.**

Okay, sure

**Seohyeon**   (40분 후) **기사님, 감사합니다.** _____. ❸

(40 minutes later) Thank you, driver. Please let me off here.

---

### Answer

❶ Please go to Lotte World. Is it far from here?
  롯데월드로 가 주세요. 여기에서 먼가요?
❷ Can you go faster, please?   빨리 가 주실 수 있으세요?
❸ Please let me off here.   여기에서 세워 주세요.

TRACK 33

# 공항으로 가는 버스는 몇 번이에요?
**Which bus goes to the airport?**

✏️ **Do you want to know How to get around by bus?**

Before taking the bus, you need to check the number of the buses you need to take to reach your destination. You can find this information directly at the bus stops, since most bus stops have the line number written on the walls. But if you look at the number and are still not sure, turn to any Korean around you and say "실례합니다. (Destination)+로/으로 가는 버스는 몇 번이에요?". This means, "Excuse me. Which bus that goes to (Destination).

**Today's Pattern**

| N+로/으로 가는 버스는 | 몇 번이에요? |
|---|---|
| **공항으로 가는 버스는** | **몇 번이에요?** |
| Bus goes to the airport | what number |

**Which bus goes to the airport?**
~로/으로 가는 버스는 몇 번이에요?

**5 Key Sentences**

- 공항으로 가는 버스는 몇 번이에요? [면뻐니에요] — Which bus goes to the airport?
- 광장시장으로 가는 버스는 몇 번이에요? — Which bus goes to Gwangjang Market?
- 서울숲으로 가는 버스는 몇 번이에요? [서울수프로] — Which bus goes to Seoul Forest?
- 동대문으로 가는 버스는 몇 번이에요? — Which bus goes to Dongdaemun?
- 석촌호수로 가는 버스는 몇 번이에요? — Which bus goes to Seokchon Lake?

**Speak like a native with natural expressions**

**Take bus number 1004-1.**

**1004-1번 버스를 타세요.** 
[천사다시일번]

- 'Bus number 1004-1' is read as '1004-1번 버스' in Korean (pronounced '천사 다시 일'). You first mention the number in Korean, and then "번 버스". "번" comes from the first syllable in "번호", and means 'number'.
- 버스를 타다 get on a bus.

**Where can I buy a bus ticket?**

**버스표는 어디에서 사요?**

▷ **버스 티켓** Bus ticket

- To ride on specific buses such as airport and intercity buses, you must buy a bus ticket. But you can pay for regular buses using cash, credit card or your T-money card.

**I think I took the wrong bus.**

**버스를 잘못 탄 것 같아요.**

**Let me know when this bus arrives at the Olympic Park.**

**올림픽공원에 도착하면 좀 알려 주세요.**

- If you are worried that you will miss your stop and fail to get off, you can ask the bus driver to remind you like this. At this time, it's good to sit in the back seat or the seat close to the driver. And, remember to start your request by respectfully calling the driver '기사님'.

**How much do I owe you?**

**요금이 얼마예요?**

- If you are not sure how much the fare is, ask this question to the bus driver.

**79**

**Does this bus go to Hongdae?**　이 버스가 홍대로 가나요? ◁€

- If you want to make sure of the destination the bus is heading towards, use this expression to check with the bus driver.

**Where do I get off to get to Seongsu Station?**　성수역에 가려면 어디에서 내려야 돼요? ◁€

**Go one more stop and you can get off**　한 정거장 더 가서 내리세요. ◁€

▸ **다음 정거장에서** at the next stop

**We are not going to Hongdae.**　홍대 안 갑니다. ◁€

- If you ask whether the bus is going to Hongdae and get this response, it means that the bus route does not include Hongdae (it's not that the driver does not want to go there).

**Transfer to bus number 67 at the next stop.**　다음 정거장에서 67번 버스로 갈아타세요. ◁€

▸ **정류장** bus stop
- 정류장=정거장
- 갈아타다/환승하다 transfer

Write down the appropriate sentence in the blank space and practice your pronunciations by reading out loud.

---

**Minjun**

**실례합니다. 뭐 좀 여쭤 볼 게 있는데요.**

Excuse me. I need to ask you something.

**Passerby**

**네, 말씀하세요.**

Yes, go ahead.

**Minjun**

_____ ? ❶

Which bus goes to Seoul Forest?

**Passersby**

**잠시만요,** (노선표 확인 후) _____ . ❷

Hold on, (After checking the bus route) take the number 101

bus.

**Minjun**

**감사합니다. 혹시,** _____ ? ❸

Thank you. By any chance, how much is the fare?

---

**Passersby**

**1,200원이에요.**

It's 1,200 won.

---

 **Answer**

❶ Which bus goes to Seoul Forest? 서울숲으로 가는 버스는 몇 번이에요?

❷ Take the number 101 bus. 101번 버스를 타세요.

❸ How much do I owe you? 요금이 얼마예요?

TRACK 35

# 신촌까지 지하철로 어떻게 가요?
How can I get to Sinchon by subway?

 **Do you want to know** How to get around by using the subway?

As of May 28, 2022, there are 11 subway (지하철) lines running in Seoul. Regardless of your destination, you can easily and safely reach your destination using the Seoul subway. However, getting to your destination on just one ride, without changing subways, only happens if you are lucky. Therefore, you need to know how to get there accurately. You can for direction or information by using this sentence pattern: '(destination)까지 지하철로 어떻게 가요?'. Of course, this pattern can also be used with other types of public transport besides the subway.

## Today's **Pattern**

| N+까지 | N+로/으로 | 어떻게 가요? |
|---|---|---|
| **신촌까지** | **지하철로** | **어떻게 가요?** |
| to Sinchon | by subway | how can I get |

**How can I get to Sinchon by subway?**
~까지 ~로/으로 어떻게 가요?

## 5 Key Sentences

- 신촌까지 지하철로 어떻게 가요?    How can I get to Sinchon by subway?
- 이대까지 지하철로 어떻게 가요?    How can I get to Ewha Women's University by subway?
- 명동까지 지하철로 어떻게 가요?    How can I get to Myeongdong by subway?
- 인천공항까지 지하철로 어떻게 가요?    How do I get to Incheon Airport by subway?
- 롯데타워까지 지하철로 어떻게 가요?    How can I get to Lotte Tower by subway?

**Speak like a native with natural expressions**

### It's pretty close/ It's quite close

패 가까워요. 🔊

▸ **멀어요** far

● This is the most basic expression used when talking about distances. It is very useful so be sure to remember it!

### It's a five-minute walk.

걸어서 5분 거리예요. 🔊
[거러서오분]

▸ **10분** 10 minutes

● 걸어서 on foot
● 거리 distance

### Get off through at exit 2.

2번 출구로 나가세요. 🔊
[이번]

▸ **8번** no. 8

● On average, most Seoul subway stations have at least 4 exits. If perhaps you have to meet someone at the subway station, make sure to check what exit number you will meet at.

### Follow the green arrow.

녹색 화살표를 따라가세요. 🔊

▸ **파란색** blue
▸ **오렌지색** orange

● Are you worried about reaching your next transfer point after getting off the subway? It's not difficult, so don't worry. Each subway line has a designated colour, so just follow the coloured arrows.

### Get off at the next station.

다음 역에서 내리세요. 🔊
[다음녀게서]00000000000000000

▸ **신도림역** Sindorim station
▸ **교대역** Korea University station

**Is it within a walking distance from the hotel to the subway station?**

호텔에서 지하철역까지 걸어갈 수 있나요? 🔊

▸ **명동역에서 명동 성당** from Myeongdong station to Myeongdong Cathedral

● Most tourist sites are within walking distance from a subway station. But sometimes that can mean a very long walk. In such cases, just take the bus in front of the subway station.

**What time is the last bus to Gangnam Station?**

강남역으로 가는 막차는 몇 시에 있어요? 🔊

▸ **첫차** first bus

**Which exit do I have to go out?**

몇 번 출구로 나가야 돼요? 🔊
[멷 뻔]

**Transfer to Line 5 at Jongno 3-ga Station.**

종로 3가역에서 5호선으로 갈아타세요. 🔊

▸ **강남역에서 신분당선**

● The most recently created subway lines have names instead of numbers, eg. Shinbundang line (신분당선), Airport railway (공항철도), Everline (에버라인), Wuyi foundation (우이신설), Gimpo Gold (김포골드) etc.

**Take Line 2 from here to Ewha Womans University Station.**

여기에서 2호선을 타고 이대역까지 가세요. 🔊

▸ **합정역** Hapjeong station

Write down the appropriate sentence in the blank space and practice your pronunciations by reading out loud.

Sooah _____? ❶

How can I get to Ewha Womans University by subway?

Guide **여기에서 2호선을 타고 이대역까지 가세요.**

Take Line 2 from here to Ewha Womans University Station.

Sooah **이대역에서 이대까지 걸어갈 수 있나요?**

Can I walk from that Station to Ewha Womans University?

Guide **네, 가까워요.** _____. ❷

Yes, it's nearby. It's a five-minute walk.

Sooah _____? ❸

Which exit should I take?

Guide **2번 출구로 나가세요.**

Go out through exit 2.

**Answer**

❶ How can I get to Ewha Womans University by subway?
  이대까지 지하철로 어떻게 가요?
❷ It's a five-minute walk.    걸어서 5분 거리예요.
❸ Which exit should I take?    몇 번 출구로 나가야 돼요?

TRACK 37

# 부산행 8시 기차표 있나요?
## Do you have an 8 o'clock train ticket to Busan?

 **Do you want to know** How to get around the railway station?

In Korea, 'subways' are only found in big cities such as Seoul. Therefore, when traveling from Seoul to very far places, you have to take a train (기차), an express bus (고속버스), or take a domestic (국내) flight from Gimpo Airport. Because 'train' and 'subway' refer to different modes of transportations in Korea; be sure to understand the difference. In today's lesson, let's take a look at some expressions you can use when in a railway (train) station.

---

**Today's Pattern**

| N(city)+행 | Ad(Time) | 기차표 있나요? |
|---|---|---|
| **부산행** | **8시** | **기차표 있나요?** |
| to Busan | 8 o'clock | Do you have a rail ticket? |

**Do you have an 8 o'clock train ticket to Busan?**
~행 ~시 기차표 있나요?

---

**5 Key** **Sentences**

- **부산행 8시 기차표 있나요?**    Do you have an 8 o'clock train ticket to Busan?
- **전주행 5시 기차표 있나요?**    Do you have any 5 o'clock train tickets to Jeonju?
- **여수행 6시 기차표 있나요?**    Do you have any 6 o'clock train tickets to Yeosu?
- **남해행 12시 기차표 있나요?**    Do you have a 12 o'clock train ticket to Namhae?
- **울산행 2시 기차표 있나요?**    Do you have a 2 o'clock train ticket to Ulsan?

**Speak like a native with natural expressions**

**Where's the ticket office?**

매표소가 어디에 있어요? ◁

▸ **열차 타는 곳이** (boarding) platform
▸ **열차 내리는 곳이** (disembarking) platform
● 기차=열차 train

**Where can I buy a ticket?**

어디에서 표를 끊어야 될까요? ◁
　　　　　[끄너야]

▸ **표를 사야** can buy a ticket
● 표를 끊다=표를 사다 buy a ticket

**When does the next KTX to Busan depart?**

부산 가는 다음 KTX는 언제 출발해요? ◁

● KTX is the abbreviation for Korea Train Express. On the KTX, you can get from Seoul station to Busan station in two and a half or three hours.

**It takes about two and a half hours.**

두 시간 반 정도 걸려요. ◁

**I missed the train. Can I get a refund?**

기차를 놓쳤는데 환불받을 수 있나요? ◁
　　　　　[노천는데]

● If you miss your train, you can get a refund at the ticketing office. Refund charges can range from at least 15% after train departure to 70% at most after train arrival.

**Please give me the earliest train ticket.**

가장 빨리 출발하는 걸로 주세요. ◁
　　　　　[출바라는]

**How long does it take to get to Jeonju?**　전주까지 얼마나 걸려요? 🔊

**At which platform do I take the train to Yeosu?**　여수 가는 기차는 몇 번 승강장에서 타요? 🔊

**I'd like a window seat, please.**　창가쪽 자리로 주세요. 🔊

▸ **안쪽 자리로** inside seating
▸ **입석으로** standing room

**Is there a Mugunghwa train bound for Daejeon tomorrow morning?**　내일 아침에 출발하는 대전행 무궁화호 있나요? 🔊

▸ **내일 오전에** tomorrow before noon
▸ **12시 넘어서** after 12
▸ **오후에** afternoon

● Presently, in Korea, operating trains can be divided into several categories based on their speed, destination etc. Among express trains, there are KTX and SRT, while the regular passenger trains include Mugunghwa and Saemaeul.

## Speak with me

Write down the appropriate sentence in the blank space and practice your pronunciations by reading out loud.

---

**Siwoo**          _____? ❶

Do you have an 8 o'clock train ticket to Busan?

**Ticket office staff**  **네, 8시에 출발하는 KTX가 있습니다.**

Yes, there is a KTX departing at 8 o'clock.

**Siwoo**          **KTX로** _____? ❷

How long does it take to get to Busan by KTX?

**Ticket office staff**  _____. ❸

It takes about 2 hours and 45 minutes.

**Siwoo**          **그럼 그걸로 한 장 주세요. 얼마예요?**

Alright, I'd like one of those. How much is it?

**Ticket office staff**  **59,800원 입니다.**

It's 59,800 won.

---

**Answer**

❶ Do you have an 8 o'clock train ticket to Busan?   부산행 8시 기차표
있나요?
❷ How long does it take to Busan?         부산까지 얼마나 걸려요?
❸ It takes about 2 hours and 45 minutes.      2시간 45분 정도 걸려요.

TRACK 39

# 환전소가 어디예요?
## Where is the currency exchange?

 **Do you want to know** How to get around the airport?

Have you ever been to Incheon Airport? If you plan to visit Korea, the first place you will arrive at is the airport. With all your excitement, you will have to leave the airport and get on the subway, airport bus or a taxi to get to your next destination. Or perhaps, you may want to exchange money, get a T-money card or buy a sim card. So, for today let's go over Korean expressions that you can use at the airport.

---

**Today's Pattern**

| N+이/가 | 어디예요? |
|---|---|
| **환전소가** | **어디예요?** |
| the currency exchange counter | Where is |

**Where is the currency exchange?**
~이/가 어디예요?

---

**5 Key** **Sentences**

- **환전소가 어디예요?**     Where is the currency exchange?
- **관광 안내 센터가 어디예요?**     Where is the tourist information center?
- **짐 찾는 곳이 어디예요?**     Where is the baggage claim area?
  [찬는고시]
- **지하철 타는 곳이 어디예요?**     Where is the subway station?
- **티머니 카드 파는 곳이 어디예요?**     Where can I buy T-money cards?

**Speak like a native with natural expressions** 🎧

**Where is the information center?**

안내 센터는 어디에 있어요? 🔊

▸ **수하물 보관소** baggage claim area

**Where should I go to take the subway?**

지하철을 타려면 어디로 가야 돼요? 🔊
[지아처를/지하처를]

▸ **공항철도를** airport train
▸ **공항버스를** airport bus

**Where can I buy a sim card?**

심카드는 어디에서 살 수 있어요? 🔊

▸ **티머니 카드는** T-money card
▸ **승차권은** ticket

● The T-money card is a transit card that can be used on the bus, subway, and even in taxis. You recharge your card with the amount you want, and the trip fare is taken based on your usage time.

**It's next to Gate 4.**

4번 게이트 옆에 있어요. 🔊
[사번]

**Which bus do I take to get to Jongno?**

종로에 가려면 몇 번 버스를 타야 돼요? 🔊

**Take bus no. 6001 or 6015.**

6001번이나 6015번 버스를 타세요. 🔊
[육천일번]    [육천시보번]

● 이나 or

**Where can I get a tax refund?**

세금 환급은 어디에서 받을 수 있어요? 🔊

**Buy it from a Kiosk ticketing machine.**

무인발권기에서 구입하세요. 🔊

● 무인 無人 unmanned(unstaffed)

**91**

Go to the Seoul Tourism Information Center in front of Exit 10 on the first floor.

1층의 10번 출구 앞에 있는
[일층에십뻔]
서울관광정보센터로 가세요.

I'd like a 10,000 won card, please.

10000원 짜리로 하나 주세요.
[마눤]

▸ **5000원 짜리** 5000 won value
[오처눤]

- 짜리 a suffix that adds the meaning of 'something with that number or amount' or 'something with that value

Write down the appropriate sentence in the blank space and practice your pronunciations by reading out loud.

(At the airport information desk)

**Info desk attendant**　무엇을 도와 드릴까요?

How may I help you?

**Jennifer**　네, _____? ❶

Yes, where is the subway station?

**Info desk attendant**　지하 1층으로 내려가시면 됩니다.
공항철도 표지판을 따라가세요.

You can go down to B1F. Then, follow the airport rail-road sign.

**Jennifer**　_____? ❷

Where can I buy a T-money card?

**Info desk attendant**　여기에서 살 수 있으세요. 하나 드릴까요?

You can buy it here. Would you like one?

**Jennifer**　네, _____. ❸

Yes, I'd like a 10,000 won card, please.

### Answer

❶ Where is the subway station?　　지하철 타는 곳이 어디예요?
❷ Where can I buy a T-money card?　티머니 카드는 어디에서 살 수 있어요?
❸ I'd like a 10,000 won card, please.　10000원 짜리로 주세요.

TRACK 41

# 여기에서 박물관까지 가까운가요?

**Is the museum nearby?**

 **Do you want to know** How to find your way around the streets?

It's easy to get lost, especially trying to read a map in unfamiliar locations. At such times, it can be very helpful to ask a passerby for directions. Today, we will learn how to talk to someone on the street and the helpful expressions to use when asking for directions and distance. They are very useful, so pay close attention!

## Today's **Pattern**

| 여기에서 | N+까지 | 가까운가요? |
|---|---|---|
| **여기에서** | **박물관까지** | **가까운가요?** |
| from here | to the museum | Is it close? |

**Is the museum nearby?**
여기에서 ~까지 가까운가요?

## 5 Key Sentences

- **여기에서 박물관까지 가까운가요?**　　Is the museum nearby?
  [방물관]
- **여기에서 코스트코까지 가까운가요?**　Is this place close to Costco?
- **여기에서 클럽까지 가까운가요?**　　Are we getting closer to the club?
- **여기에서 화장실까지 가까운가요?**　Is the bathroom nearby?
- **여기에서 놀이공원까지 가까운가요?**　Is this place close to the amusement park?
  [노리공원]

**Speak like a native with natural expressions**

**Can I walk to the Han River from here?**

여기에서 한강까지 걸어갈 수 있나요?
[거러갈쑤인나요]

**Is it far from the station to Lotte World?**

역에서 롯데월드까지 멀어요?

▸ **여기에서 공원까지** from here to the park
▸ **호텔에서 공연장까지** from the hotel to the concert hall

**It's next to the post office.**

우체국 옆에 있어요.

▸ **앞** in front
▸ **오른쪽** right side
▸ **왼쪽** left side
▸ **건너편** opposite side
▸ **뒤쪽** behind

**It's a long way to walk.**

걸어가기에는 멀어요.

**It's pretty close.
It's a five-minute walk.**

꽤 가까워요. 걸어서 5분 거리예요.

▸ **차로** by car
▸ **버스로** by bus
▸ **지하철로** by subway

**How do I get there?**

거기까지 어떻게 가야 돼요?

**Go straight ahead.**

쭉 직진하세요.

**Is there a public restroom around here?**

이 근처에 공공 화장실이 있나요?

▸ **가까운 곳** a place close-by

● 근처 nearby
● '이 근처' and '가까운 곳' can be used interchangeably in this sentence, as they have the same meaning.

**95**

**Is this the right way to the Deoksugung Palace?**

우리가 덕수궁으로 맞게 가고 있나요? 🔊

▸ **잘** right


**Keep walking forward after reaching the bank.**

은행을 지나서 계속 가세요. 🔊
[으냉]

▸ **조금만 더** only a bit more

Write down the appropriate sentence in the blank space and practice your pronunciations by reading out loud.

(at the airport information desk)

**Siwoo** _____ ? ❶

Is there a 'Champ coffee' near here?

**Passerby** 네, 게스트 하우스 앞에 있어요.

Yes, it's in front of the guest house.

**Siwoo** _____ ? ❷

Is it close from here?

**Passerby** 꽤 가까워요. 걸어서 5분 거리예요.

It's pretty close. It's a five-minute walk.

**Siwoo** _____ ? ❸

How do I get there?

**Passerby** 길을 건너서, 저 아래로 쭉 직진하세요.

Cross the street, then go straight from there.

**Answer**

❶ Is there a 'Champ coffee' near here?    이 근처에 '챔프 커피'가 있나요?
❷ Is it close from here?    여기에서 가까운가요??
❸ How do I get there?    거기까지 어떻게 가야 돼요?

# UNIT 4

# Emergencies

TRACK 43

# 머리가 아파요.

**I have a headache.**

 **Do you want to know How to describe ailments at the hospital?**

I hope that you remain healthy while in Korea. However, at times we may come across unpredictable health problems while traveling abroad. In today's lesson, we will look at some basic expressions you can use to explain your symptoms. Of course, the best scenario would be an English-speaking doctor, but if you can't find one, or need to go to a hospital you might need to know some of these sentences. Let's practice together.

### Today's **Pattern**

| N+이/가 | 아파요. |
|---------|---------|
| **머리가** | **아파요.** |
| a head | hurts |

**I have a headache.**
~이/가 아파요

### 5 Key Sentences

- **머리가 아파요.**     I have a headache.
- **배가 아파요.**     I've got a bellyache.
- **목이 아파요.**     My neck hurts/My throat is sore.
- **이가 아파요.**     I have a toothache.
- **다리가 아파요.**     My legs are hurting.

**Speak like a native with natural expressions**

| | |
|---|---|
| **Do you have any doctors who speak English?** | 영어 하시는 의사 선생님 계세요? ◁€ |

| | |
|---|---|
| **My back has always been in bad shape.** | 원래 허리가 안 좋아요. ◁€<br>[월래] |

▶ **피부가** skin
▶ **손목이** wrist

● You can talk about any pre-existing symptoms you have using this expression.

| | |
|---|---|
| **I have a fever.** | 열이 있어요. ◁€ |

▶ **알레르기가** Allergy
▶ **두통이** Headache
▶ **근육통이** Muscle pain/cramps

| | |
|---|---|
| **I have a cough.** | 기침이 나와요. ◁€ |

▶ **재채기가** Sneezing
▶ **콧물이** Runny nose.

| | |
|---|---|
| **I have hurt my back.** | 허리를 다쳤어요. ◁€ |

▶ **다리를** leg
▶ **팔을** arm

| | |
|---|---|
| **I feel dizzy.** | 머리가 어지러워요. ◁€ |

| | |
|---|---|
| **Please tell me your name and date of birth.** | 성함과 생년월일을 알려 주세요. ◁€ |

● During your first visit to a hospital, it is common for the staff to ask for your basic personal information. If more detailed information is needed, you will be given documents to fill out.

**101**

**What brings you here?**　　　어떻게 오셨어요? ◁€
　　　　　　　　　　　　　　　　[오셔써요]

- This is something the doctor will ask at the beginning of your consultation.

**When did it start?**　　　언제부터 아프셨어요? ◁€

- In other words, it can also be said, '언제부터 증상이 있으셨어요?' 증상 means 'symptoms'.

**I've been sick since yesterday.**　　어제부터 아팠어요. ◁€

- ▸ **오늘 아침** this morning
- ▸ **이틀 전** two days ago
- ▸ **일주일 전** a week ago

## Speak with me

Write down the appropriate sentence in the blank space and practice your pronunciations by reading out loud.

| | |
|---|---|
| **Doctor** | **어떻게 오셨어요?** |
| | What brings you here? |
| **Minjun** | _____ . ❶ |
| | I have a headache. |
| **Doctor** | **언제부터 아프셨어요?** |
| | When did it start? |
| **Minjun** | _____ . ❷ **원래 두통이 있어요.** |
| | I've been sick since this morning. I often have a headache. |
| **Doctor** | **다른 아픈 데는 없으세요?** |
| | Are you sick anywhere else? |
| **Minjun** | _____ . ❸ |
| | I also have a fever. |

**Answer**

❶ I have a headache. 머리가 아파요.
❷ I've been sick since this morning. 오늘 아침부터 아팠어요.
❸ I also have a fever. 열도 있어요.

TRACK 45

# 도와주세요. 차 사고가 났어요.

## Please help. There's been a car accident.

 **Do you want to know How to make a report to the police?**

Korea is known as one of the safest countries for travellers. But if there is an emergency, you have to call the police as fast as possible. Once you dial the number 112, you will immediately be connected to the police. As calmly as you possibly can, explain your emergency, and most importantly, give them your location too. Let's take a look at how to do this in today's lesson.

---

### Today's Pattern

| 도와주세요. | Situation |
|:---:|:---:|
| **도와주세요.** | **차 사고가 났어요.** |
| **Please help.** | **There's been a car accident.** |

**Please help. There's been a car accident.**
도와주세요.+ Situation

---

### 5 Key Sentences

- **도와주세요. 차 사고가 났어요.**
  Please help. There's been a car accident.

- **도와주세요. 누가 절 쫓아와요.**
  [쫓차와요]
  Please help. Someone keeps chasing me.

- **도와주세요. 술 취한 사람이 괴롭혀요.**
  [괴로펴요]
  Please help. Drunk people are bothering me.

- **도와주세요. 성폭행하려고 해요.**
  [성포캥]
  Please help. A man is trying to assault me.

- **도와주세요. 도둑을 신고하고 싶어요.**
  Please help. I want to report a theft.

**Speak like a native with natural expressions**

**It's an emergency.**

긴급 상황이에요.
[긴급상황]

▸ **응급 상황** emergency

● If trying to help someone who has been seriously injured, call 119 and say, "응급 상황이에요", then let them know your location.

**Please come quickly.**

빨리 와 주세요.

**What's your current location?**

현재 위치가 어떻게 되세요?

**It's in the playground in front of Hongdae.**

홍대 앞 놀이터에 있어요.

● It is important to give your location when making a report. Check for a signpost or the number of the telephone pole close to you, and tell the police officer.

**There is a traffic accident.**

교통사고가 났어요.

● You can say '사고가 났어요' when reporting any type of accident, including traffic accidents.

**Someone broke into my house.**

누가 제 집에 침입했어요.
[치미패써요]

▸ **침입하다** break-in

**It's a rapist.**

강간범이에요.

▸ **도둑** thief, theft

**A drunken man is making a scene on the street.**

술 취한 사람이 길에서 난동을 부리고 있어요.

● 난동을 부리다 go on a rampage

**I'd like to report a stalker.**

스토커를 신고하려고요. 🔊

▸ **방화범을** arsonist
▸ **강도를** robber

**Someone's coming after me!
Please hide me!**

누가 절 쫓아와요! 저 좀 숨겨 주세요! 🔊

● If you are a woman and are being chased at night by a strange person, enter the shop nearest to you and ask for help. If there is no time to call the police, it is best to run to somewhere bright, with many people present.

Write down the appropriate sentence in the blank space and practice your pronunciations by reading out loud.

**Police**  **하기 파출소입니다.**
Hagi police box.

**Sooah**  _____. ❶
Help me. There is a drunken man going on a rampage.

**Police**  **현재 위치가 어떻게 되세요?**
What's your current location?

**Sooah**  _____. ❷
It is next to Sora Elementary School.

**Police**  **대로변인가요?**
Is it at a roadside?

**Sooah**  **네,** _____. ❸
Yes, in front of the GS convenience store.

---

**Answer**

❶ Help me. There is a drunken man going on a rampage.
도와주세요. 술 취한 사람이 난동을 부리고 있어요.

❷ It is next to Sora Elementary School.  소라 초등학교 옆이에요.

❸ In front of the GS convenience store.  GS 편의점 앞이에요.

TRACK 47

# 아플 때만 드세요.

**Only take it when you are sick.**

 **Do you want to know How to get medicine at the pharmacy?**

When traveling, be sure to carry some common medication with you. In case if you run out of indigestion or nausea while traveling, you can go to a pharmacy to get what you need. Or perhaps, you need some fever medicine or painkillers late at night; you can go to a convenience store to get them. These common medicines are on display, so you can easily buy them. Let's practice some expressions you can use while at a pharmacy.

---

**Today's Pattern**

| Ad(time) | 드세요. |
|---|---|
| **아플 때만** | **드세요.** |
| **only when you are sick** | **Take it** |

**Only take it when you are sick.**
~드세요.

---

**5 Key** **Sentences**

- **아플 때만 드세요.**    Only take it when you are sick.
- **식전에 드세요.**    Please take it before a meal.
  [식쩌네]
- **식후에 드세요.**    Please take it after a meal.
  [시쿠에]
- **공복에 드세요.**    Take it on an empty stomach.
- **하루에 세 번 드세요.**    Take it three times a day.

**Speak like a native with natural expressions**

**Do you have any pain relievers?** 진통제 있어요?

▸ **소화제** digestion medicine
▸ **해열제** fever medication/antipyretics

**I'd like a fast-acting one.** 효과 빠른 걸로 주세요.

▸ **센 걸** strong one
[쎈걸]

**Take one pill at a time.** 한 알씩 드세요.
[하날]

▸ **두 알** two pills
● The counter '알' can be used interchangeably with '개', so that you have '한 알' or '한 개', '두 알'or '두 개'.

**Do I have to take it after a meal?** 식후에 먹어야 하나요?

**How should I take it?** 어떻게 먹어야 돼요?

● Use this expression to ask how to take the medication.

**It doesn't matter, you can take it on an empty stomach or after meals.** 공복에 드셔도 상관없어요.

▸ **아무때나 드셔도** take it anytime
● In the pattern, '아/어도 상관없다', it means that whatever is in front of '아/어도' does not affect the end result.

**Does it have any side effects?** 어떤 부작용이 있을 수 있나요?

**It may cause you slight dizziness.** 약간 어지러울 수도 있어요.

▸ **메스꺼울 수도** could make you nauseous

**Do you have a prescription?** 처방전 있으세요? 🔊

**Can I buy it without a prescription?** 처방전 없이도 살 수 있나요? 🔊

## Speak with me

Write down the appropriate sentence in the blank space and practice your pronunciations by reading out loud.

**Siwoo** _____ ? ● 효과 빠른 걸로요.

Do you have any painkillers? I'd like a fast-acting one.

**Pharmacist** 여기 있어요. _____ . ●

Here you go. Take one pill only when you are sick.

**Siwoo** _____ ? ●

Do I have to take it after a meal?

**Pharmacist** 아니요, 공복에 드셔도 상관없어요.

No, you take it on an empty stomach.

**Siwoo** 먹으면 졸릴 수 있나요?

Will it make me sleepy after taking it?

**Pharmacist** 그건 사람마다 다를 수 있어요.

It can vary from one person to another.

**Answer**

● Do you have any painkillers?     진통제 있어요?
● Take one pill only when you are sick.     아플 때만 한 알씩 드세요.
● Do I have to take it after a meal?     식후에 먹어야 하나요?

111

TRACK 49

# 119를 불러 주세요.

Please call 119.

 **Do you want to know How to call for an ambulance?**

In Korea, if you are seriously injured or have a medical emergency, the number to dial is 119. However, you may find it difficult to explain your situation due to the language barrier. The best option is to ask the nearest Korean to help you. In such situation, you can simply say '119를 불러주세요', meaning 'Please call 119'. Whether it is a fire or a car accident, you can call 119 for any emergencies and make a report.

### Today's **Pattern**

| N+을/를 | 불러 주세요. |
|---|---|
| **119를** | **불러 주세요.** |
| 119 | **Please call** |

**Please call 119.**
~을/를 불러 주세요.

### 5 Key Sentences

- **119를 불러 주세요.**
  [일릴구]                    Please call 119.

- **의사를 불러 주세요.**       Please call a doctor.

- **구급차를 불러 주세요.**     Please call an ambulance

- **택시를 불러 주세요.**       Please call a taxi

- **전문가를 불러 주세요.**     Please call an expert

**Speak like a native with natural expressions**

**Please help me**

도와주세요. ◁

- Use this expression when you are in a critical situation and asking a passer-by for help

**I got burnt.**

화상을 입었어요. ◁

**There was an accident.**

사고가 났어요. ◁

▸ **불이** fire

- If it is a car accident, you say '차 사고가 났어요'.

**Are you okay?**

괜찮으세요? ◁

- This is the first thing you ask when trying to make sure that someone is not injured.

**I was bleeding a lot.**

피를 많이 흘렸어요. ◁

- *피를 흘리다: to bleed

**There is someone inside the car.**

차 안에 사람이 있어요. ◁

▸ **건물** building

**I was attacked.**

공격을 당했어요. ◁

▸ **강도를** robbery

**Please take me to the hospital.**

병원에 데려다 주세요. ◁

▸ **호텔에** to the hotel
▸ **대사관에** to the embassy

- You use this when you ask someone to take or drive you somewhere.

**113**

**I have traveller's insurance**   여행자 보험에 들었어요. 🔊

**I was seriously injured**   많이 다쳤어요. 🔊

- ▸ **머리를** head
- ▸ **눈을** eyes

Write down the appropriate sentence in the blank space and practice your pronunciations by reading out loud.

**Minjun** _____. ❶

Help me.

**Passersby** 무슨 일이세요?

What's the matter?

**Minjun** _____. ❷ 차 안에 사람이 있어요.

There is a car accident. Someone is in the car.

**Passersby** 네? 어디에서요?

What? Where is it?

**Minjun** 저쪽에서요. _____. ❸

Over there. Please call 119.

**Passersby** 큰일났네, 알겠으니까 같이 가 봐요.

Oh no, I can see it. Let's go together.

---

**Answer**

❶ Help me.                           도와주세요.
❷ There is a car accident.        차 사고가 났어요.
❸ Please call 119.                   119를 불러 주세요.

TRACK 51

# 지갑을 잃어버렸어요.
I lost my wallet.

 **Do you want to know** How to report a lost item?

Have you ever lost anything while travelling abroad? It can be much more embarrassing than losing things in your own country. However, if you know where you lost something, there is a high possibility of finding it. So don't worry. Practice saying this: '~을 잃어버렸어요.'

---

**Today's Pattern**

| N+을/를 | 잃어버렸어요. |
|---|---|
| **지갑을** | **잃어버렸어요.** |
| my wallet | I lost |

**I lost my wallet.**
~을/를 잃어버렸어요.

---

**5 Key** **Sentences**

- **지갑을 잃어버렸어요.**
  [이러버려써요]
  I lost my wallet.

- **가방을 잃어버렸어요.**
  I lost my bag.

- **스마트폰을 잃어버렸어요.**
  I lost my (smart)phone.

- **귀걸이를 잃어버렸어요.**
  I lost my earrings.

- **우산을 잃어버렸어요.**
  I lost my umbrella.

**Speak like a native with natural expressions**

| | |
|---|---|
| **I lost my smartphone here.** | 여기에서 스마트폰을 잃어버렸어요. |

**What colour is your wallet?**　지갑이 <u>무슨 색</u>이에요?
  ▸ **무슨 브랜드** what brand

**It is red.**　<u>빨간색</u>이에요.
  ▸ **까만색** black
  ▸ **갈색** brown
  ▸ **하얀색** white
  ▸ **핑크색** pink
  ▸ **노란색** yellow

**What is inside the bag?**　가방 안에 뭐가 들어 있어요?
  ● In this sentence, the words '들어 있어요', 'and '있어요' have the same meaning and can be interchanged.

**I have your wallet with me, customer.**　손님 지갑은 보관하고 있어요.
  ● 손님 customer

**I left my umbrella here.**　<u>여기에</u> 우산을 두고 갔어요.
  ▸ **지하철에** subway
  ▸ **식당에** restaurant

**Can you please check if a bag was found?**　혹시 <u>분실된 가방</u>이 들어왔는지 봐 주실래요?
  ▸ **분실물** lost property
  ● 분실되다 to be lost
  ● 분실물 lost property

**117**

**I think I left my jacket there before coming here.**

거기에 <u>재킷을</u> 두고 온 것 같아요. 🔊

▹ **모자를** hat, cap
▹ **장갑을** gloves

**If you find my wallet by any chance, can you give me a call?**

혹시 지갑을 찾으시면 여기로 전화 주시겠어요? 🔊

**I will go to find it now**

<u>지금</u> 찾으러 갈게요. 🔊

▹ **30분 뒤에** In 30 minutes
▹ **내일** tomorrow

Write down the appropriate sentence in the blank space and practice your pronunciations by reading out loud.

Seohyeon         _____. ❶

I lost my black wallet here.

Employee      _____? ❷

What brand is your wallet?

Seohyeon         **루이 비통이요.**

Louis Vuitton.

Employee      **성함이 어떻게 되세요?**

What's your name?

Seohyeon         **이서현이에요.**

It's Lee Seohyeon

Employee      _____. ❸

I have your wallet with me.

---

## Answer

❶ I lost my black wallet here.     여기에서 까만색 지갑을 잃어버렸어요.

❷ What brand is your wallet?     지갑이 무슨 브랜드예요?

❸ I have your wallet with me.     손님 지갑은 보관하고 있어요.

TRACK 53

# 침대 시트가 더러워요.
## The sheets are dirty.

 **Do you want to know How to make a complaint in the hotel?**

Upon reaching and checking into a hotel after a long journey, all you can think of is getting a much-needed rest. However, you may find yourself in an unpleasant or undesirable situation; for example, the bed sheets are dirty or the toilet is not flushing properly. What should you do? You can notify or make a complaint at the Reception Desk. Today, we will learn expressions you can use when making a complaint in the hotel or reporting an urgent situation.

### Today's Pattern

| N+이/가 | Adj/V+아/어요. |
|---|---|
| **침대 시트가** | **더러워요.** |
| **The sheets** | **are dirty** |

**The sheets are dirty.**
~이/가 ~아/어요.

### 5 Key Sentences

- **침대 시트가 더러워요.**　　　The sheets are dirty.
- **온수가 안 나와요.**　　　The hot water isn't running.
- **변기가 막혔어요.**　　　The toilet is clogged.
  [마켜써요]
- **옆방이 시끄러워요.**　　　The room next door is noisy.
  [엽빵이]
- **에어컨이 고장났어요.**　　　The air conditioner is broken.

**Speak like a native with natural expressions**

**There is a stain on the sheets** 시트에 얼룩이 있어요. ◁

● 얼룩 stain

**Could you change the sheets please?** 시트를 갈아 주시겠어요? ◁

▸ 바꿔 to change
● '시트를 갈다' and '시트를 바꾸다' can be used interchangeably.

**Could you give me more bath towels, please?** 수건을 더 주실 수 있나요? ◁

▸ 컵을 cup
▸ 물을 water

**Could you wait for a moment please?** 조금만 기다려 주시겠어요? ◁

**I don't know how to use the key card.** 카드키를 어떻게 쓰는지 모르겠어요. ◁

▸ 넷플릭스를 어떻게 보는지 how to switch on to Netflix
▸ 에어컨을 어떻게 켜는지 how to turn on the AC

**The room is too cold** 방이 너무 추워요. ◁

▸ 더워요 hot

**Can you move me to another room?** 다른 방으로 바꿔 주시겠어요? ◁

▸ 룸 room
● '룸' is used to say 'room' almost as much as '방' is use.

**The electricity isn't working.**   전기가 안 들어와요. ◁╳

▷ **불이** light

● '불이 안 들어오다' means that the lights are not working, and the opposite is '불이 들어오다', meaning 'the lights work'.

**How long should I wait?**   얼마나 기다리면 될까요? ◁╳

**Please fix it as soon as you can.**   빨리 해결 부탁드립니다. ◁╳

Write down the appropriate sentence in the blank space and practice your pronunciations by reading out loud.

**Minjun**    **여기 703호인데요.** _____. ❶

703, here. The hot water isn't running.

**Employee**    **네, 불편하게 해 드려서 죄송합니다. 현재 물탱크에 문제가 생겨서요.**

I'm sorry for the inconvenience. There's a problem with the water tank.

**조금만 기다려 주시겠어요?**

Can you wait for a little while?

**Minjun**    **아,** _____? ❷

Oh, how long do I have to wait?

**Employee**    **최대한 30분 내로 연락 드리겠습니다.**

I'll get back to you in 30 minutes at most.

**Minjun**    **그럼,** _____. ❸

Well, please fix it as fast as you can.

**Employee**    **네, 이해해 주셔서 감사합니다.**

Yes, thank you for your understanding.

**Answer**

❶ The hot water isn't running.    온수가 안 나와요.
❷ How long do I have to wait?    얼마나 기다리면 될까요?
❸ Please fix it as fast as you can.    빨리 해결 부탁드립니다.

관광 안내소
WELCOME TO KOREA

TOURIST GUIDE

# UNIT 5

# Travel

TRACK 55

# 체크인할게요.

I'd like to check in.

 **Do you want to know How to check in at a hotel?**

When travelling, your lodging is as important as the destination of your travel. Nowadays, it is very common to make reservations online, but the check in process still needs to be done in person at the accommodation of your choice. Today, we will take a look at some common expressions you can use when checking in at a hotel, or asking about service/operational hours.

---

**Today's Pattern**

| N(+로/으로) | 할게요. |
|---|---|
| **체크인** | **할게요.** |
| check in | I'd like to |

**I'd like to check in.**
~할게요.

---

**5 Key** **Sentences**

- **체크인할게요.**      I'd like to check in.
- **체크아웃할게요.**      I'd like to check out, please.
- **싱글베드로 할게요.**      I prefer a single bed.
- **오션뷰로 할게요.**      I'd like a room with an ocean view
- **더블룸으로 할게요.**      I'd like a double, please.

- The expression '~으로 할게요' indicates that there are several options, and you would like to choose one from the available options.

**Speak like a native with natural expressions**

Do you have a reservation?

예약하셨나요? ◁₭

I have a reservation under
Charlie.

찰리로 예약했어요. ◁₭
[예야캐써요]

▹ **미리** beforehand

How much is the rood charge
per night?

1박에 얼마예요? ◁₭
[일박]

▹ **하룻밤** one night
[하루빰]

Please give me a room with a
view of the river.

리버뷰로 해 주세요. ◁₭

▹ **시티뷰** a city view
▹ **마운틴뷰** a mountain view

May I have your passport,
please?

여권 좀 주시겠어요? ◁₭
[여꿘]

▹ **신분증** ID card
▹ **신용카드** Credit card

Your room number is 802.

802호로 가시면 됩니다. ◁₭

What time does the swimming
pool open?

수영장은 몇 시에 열어요? ◁₭
[며 씨]

▹ **닫아요** What time does the
swimming pool close

● 열다 to open / 닫다 to close

**127**

**Can I check in a bit earlier?**

체크인을 조금 일찍 할 수 있을까요? 🔊

**Does the room have wifi?**

방에서 와이파이 되나요? 🔊

**What time is breakfast?**

<u>조식은 언제인가요?</u> 🔊

- In hotels, the provided breakfast service is usually called '조식'(Hanja: 早食). However, instead of '조식', you may also hear '아침식사' or even '아침'. The meals provided at noon and at night are respectively called '점심' and '저녁'. Depending on the place, '런치' (lunch) and '디너'(dinner) may also be used.

Write down the appropriate sentence in the blank space and practice your pronunciations by reading out loud.

**Siwoo**   안녕하세요? _____ . ❶
Good morning, I'd like to check in.

**Employee**   예약하셨나요?
Have you made a room reservation?

**Siwoo**   네. _____ . ❷
Yes, I have a reservation under Michael.

**Employee**   _____ ? ❸
May I have your passport and credit card?

**Siwoo**   네, 여기 있어요.
Sure, here you go.

**Employee**   다 됐습니다. 507호로 가시면 됩니다.
It's done. Your room number is 507.

TRACK 57

# 영어 안내원이 있나요?
## Do you have an English-speaking guide?

 **Do you want to know** How to find an English-speaking guide?

One of the challenges when traveling abroad can be the language barrier. Therefore, it would be very helpful if tourist sites provided English-speaking guides or curators for visitors from foreign countries, wouldn't it? Currently, many famous tourist places in Korea provide English-speaking guides to assist foreign tourists. Additionally, most museums and galleries provide English audio services to guide foreign visitors around. In today's lesson, we will go over various expressions you can use to ask for services in English at tourist sites.

### Today's **Pattern**

| N+이/가 | 있나요? |
|---|---|
| **영어 안내원이** | **있나요?** |
| an English speaking guide | Do you have |

**Do you have an English–speaking guide?**
**~이/가 있나요?**

### 5 Key Sentences

- **영어 안내원이 있나요?**    Do you have an English-speaking guide?
- **영어 팜플렛이 있나요?**    Do you have a pamphlet in English?
- **영어로 된 브로슈어가 있나요?**    Do you have a brochure in English?
- **영어로 된 오디오 가이드가 있나요?**    Do you have English audio guides?
- **영어로 통역할 사람이 있나요?**    Do you have an English interpreter?
  [통역칼]

**Speak like a native with natural expressions**

**I have a question.**

여쭤볼 게 있는데요. 🔊

▸ **물어볼**

● 여쭤보다 is an honorific word for 물어보다.

**I don't understand.**

이해를 못 하겠어요. 🔊

● You can say '이해가 안 돼요' as well.

**I don't speak Korean well.**

한국어를 잘 못해요. 🔊

**Can you translate it for me, please?**

통역해 줄 수 있으세요? 🔊

**Do you have a map in English?**

영어로 나온 지도가 있나요? 🔊

▸ **팜플릿이** pamphlet

**Is the English interpreter service free?**

영어 통역 서비스는 무료인가요? 🔊

**Please translate this into Korean.**

한국어로 통역해 주세요. 🔊

▸ **중국어로** Chinese
▸ **일본어로** Japanese
▸ **프랑스어로** French
▸ **스페인어로** Spanish

**I need someone who is fluent in English.**

영어를 잘하는 사람이 필요해요. 🔊

**Please call an English interpreter for me.**

영어 통역사를 불러 주세요. 🔊

**I am looking for an English-speaking guide.**   영어로 가이드 해 줄 사람을 찾고 있어요. ◁

## Reference

- Try calling 1330 on your phone.
- 1330 is a phone and real-time chatting service that provides information on various traveling information to both domestic and foreign tourists. The service is available in Korean, English, Japanese, Chinese, Russian, Vietnamese, Thai, Malay and Indonesian.

## Speak with me

Write down the appropriate sentence in the blank space and practice your pronunciations by reading out loud.

Minjun **안녕하세요?** _____. ❶

Hello. I have a question.

Guide **네, 어떻게 도와 드릴까요?**

Yes, how can I help you?

Minjun _____? ❷

Do you have a map in English?

Guide **네, 여기 있어요. 브로슈어도 있어요.**

Sure, here you go. There's also a brochure.

Minjun _____? ❸

Is there an English-speaking guide, too?

Guide **안내원은 없는데, 오디오 서비스가 있어요.**

We don't have any guides, but we do have an audio service in English.

**Answer**

❶ I have a question. 여쭤볼 게 있는데요.

❷ Do you have a map in English? 영어로 나온 지도가 있나요?

❸ Is there an English-speaking guide, too? 영어 안내원도 있나요?

**133**

TRACK 59

# 근처에 구경할 만한 곳이 있나요?
**Are there any places to see around here?**

## Do you want to know How to ask for travel or tourist recommendations?

Have you ever met and spoken with local residents while traveling? You can get a lot of new information about interesting places to visit during your stay by having conversations with the locals; such as their favourite restaurants, popular scenic sites, or how to get discounts on tickets can be very helpful. In today's lesson, we will learn how to ask for information on local recommendations and the kinds of responses you might receive.

---

**Today's Pattern**

| 근처에 | N+이/가 | 있나요? |
|---|---|---|
| **근처에** | **구경할 만한 곳이** | **있나요?** |
| around here | any places to see | Are there |

**Are there any places to see around here?**
근처에 ~이/가 있나요?

---

**5 Key** **Sentences**

- **근처에 구경할 만한 곳이 있나요?**    Are there any places to see around here?
- **근처에 유명한 곳이 있나요?**    Are there any famous places here?
- **근처에 유명한 식당이 있나요?**    Which restaurants are famous around this area?
- **근처에 관광 안내소가 있나요?**    Is there a tourist information centre nearby?
- **근처에 역사 박물관이 있나요?**    Is there a historical museum in this area?
  [역싸방물과니]

**Speak like a native with natural expressions**

| | |
|---|---|
| **Where can I buy tickets for the city tour bus?** | 시티 투어 버스 티켓을 어디에서 살 수 있어요? 🔊 |

● Most popular cities have tour buses. If you are curious, use this expression to ask about them.

| | |
|---|---|
| **How long does the tour take?** | 투어는 얼마나 걸려요? 🔊 |

▸ 관람은 Viewing

| | |
|---|---|
| **When can I board the cruise ship?** | 유람선은 어디에서 탈 수 있어요? 🔊 |

▸ 집라인 Zip-line
[짐나인]

● Ziplines are strong, thick wire cords that are connected to supports on opposite ends, and you can move along very quickly.

| | |
|---|---|
| **What is the most famous thing in this city?** | 이 도시에서 가장 유명한 게 뭐예요? 🔊 |

● 유명하다 famous

| | |
|---|---|
| **I want to know the history of this city.** | 이 도시의 역사를 알고 싶어요. 🔊 |

[도시에 역싸]

| | |
|---|---|
| **How can I get there?** | 거기에 어떻게 갈 수 있어요? 🔊 |

| | |
|---|---|
| **Where is the souvenir shop?** | 기념품 가게는 어디에 있어요? 🔊 |

| | |
|---|---|
| **How much is the museum's entrance fee?** | 박물관 입장료가 얼마예요? 🔊 |

▸ 표가
▸ 티켓이

● 표=티켓 ticket

**Is there a student discount?** 학생 할인이 되나요? ◁

▶ **외국인** foreigner

**What are the local specialties?** 이 지역 특산물은 뭐예요? ◁

Write down the appropriate sentence in the blank space and practice your pronunciations by reading out loud.

| | |
|---|---|
| Sooah | **저기요, _____? ❶**<br>Excuse me, Are there any places to see around here? |
| Guest house employee | **순천만 가 보셨어요?**<br>Have you been to Suncheon Bay? |
| Sooah | **아니요. _____? ❷**<br>No. How can I get there? |
| Guest house employee | **순천 시티 투어 버스를 타도 되고 67번 버스를 타도 돼요.**<br>You can take the Suncheon City Tour bus or the number 67 bus. |
| Sooah | **_____? ❸**<br>Where can I buy a city bus tour ticket? |
| Guest house employee | **탑승 장소에서 기사님께 살 수 있어요.**<br>You can buy it from the driver at the boarding place. |

**Answer**

❶ Are there any places to see around here? 근처에 구경할 만한 곳이 있나요?
❷ How can I get there? 거기에 어떻게 갈 수 있어요?
❸ Where can I buy a city bus tour ticket? 시티 투어 버스 티켓을 어디에서 살 수 있어요?

TRACK 61

# 사진 좀 찍어 주시겠어요?
## Could you take a picture of me?

 **Do you want to know How to ask a stranger to take your photo?**

Do you take a lot of pictures while traveling? Nowadays, many people take selfies on their smartphones. However, if you want to take a picture with an interesting background to create new memories, you might have to ask stranger or a passer-by to take a picture for you. A pattern that is often used when requesting someone to do something is 'Verb + 아/어 주시겠어요?'. Let's practice using some frequently-used verbs.

---

### Today's **Pattern**

| N 좀 | V+아/어 주시겠어요? |
|---|---|
| **사진 좀** | **찍어 주시겠어요?** |
| a picture | Could you take a picture of |

**Could you take a picture of me?**
N 좀 V+아/어 주시겠어요?

---

### 5 Key Sentences

- **사진 좀 찍어 주시겠어요?**　　　Could you take a picture of me?
  [사진좀] [찌거주시게써요]
- **이쪽에 서 주시겠어요?**　　　　Could you stand over here, please?
- **이것 좀 들어 주시겠어요?**　　　Could you hold this for me, please?
- **제 옆에 앉아 주시겠어요?**　　　Could you sit beside me, please?
- **모자 좀 벗어 주시겠어요?**　　　Could you take off your hat, please?

**Speak like a native with natural expressions**

Am I allowed to take pictures here?

여기에서 사진을 찍어도 <u>될까요?</u> ◁

▹ 되나요?

▹ 돼요?

● The ending (어미) '~아/어도 될까요?' is most often used when asking for permission. Using '되나요' or '돼요' in place of '될까요' gives the same meaning.

Let's take a picture together.

같이 사진 찍어요. ◁

Please take a picture with that statue in the background

저 조각상을 배경으로 찍어 주세요. ◁

▹ 저 산을 That mountain

▹ 저 호수를 That lake

▹ 저 강을 That river

Does this flower show up in the picture too?

이 꽃도 같이 나오나요? ◁

▹ 이 나무도 This tree too

▹ 저 건물도 That building too

● You can use this expression when asking if something you want also appears in the picture taken.

Here we go.

자, 찍습니다. ◁

One, two, three! Kimchi!

하나, 둘, 셋, 김치! ◁

● When Koreans take pictures, they usually say "김치!(Kimchi!)" to smile.

Smile!

웃으세요! ◁

Press here.

여기를 누르면 돼요. ◁

▹ 이 버튼을 this button

**139**

**I closed my eyes.** 눈을 감았어요. 🔊

**I'll take one more picture.** 한 장만 더 찍을게요. 🔊

- This is what the photographer usually says because it's common to take two or three photos.

Write down the appropriate sentence in the blank space and practice your pronunciations by reading out loud.

**Siwoo**   저기요. _____? ❶

Excuse me. Could you take a picture of me?

**Passersby**   그럼요. 카메라 주세요.

Sure. Give me the camera.

**Siwoo**   _____? ❷

Please take a picture with that mountain in the background.

**Passersby**   아, 그럼 조금만 왼쪽으로 가 보세요.

Oh, then move to the left a bit.

**Siwoo**   _____? ❸

Does this flower show up in it too?

**Passersby**   아주 잘 나옵니다. 이제 찍습니다. 하나, 둘, 셋!

It shows up really well. I'm going to take it now. One, two, three!

**Answer**

❶ Could you take a picture of me?      사진 좀 찍어 주시겠어요?
❷ Please take a picture with that mountain in the background.
                                                      저 산을 배경으로 찍어 주세요.
❸ Does this flower show up in it too?    이 꽃도 같이 나오나요?

# UNIT 6

# Meeting new people

TRACK 63

# 안녕? 내 이름은 잭이야.

Hi, my name is Jack.

 **Do you want to know How to introduce yourself in a casual setting?**

In today's lesson, we will take a look at expressions for self-introductions (자기 소개). You might think that introducing yourself in a casual setting is simple and straightforward. Well, yes and no. This is because there are many different ways to introduce yourself in Korean, all of which I have prepared to teach you. Let's practice how to introduce oneself in informal and casual settings; e.g., when you meeting your peers at school.

---

**Today's Pattern**

| 안녕? | 내 이름은 | N+야/이야. |
|:---:|:---:|:---:|
| **안녕?** | **내 이름은** | **잭이야.** |
| **Hi,** | **My name** | **is Jack.** |

**Hi, my name is Jack.**
**안녕? 내 이름은 잭이야.**

---

**5 Key** **Sentences**

- **안녕? 내 이름은 잭이야.**     Hi, my name is Jack.
- **안녕? 내 이름은 케이티야.**     Hi, my name is Katy.
- **안녕? 내 이름은 프리야야.**     Hi, my name is Priya.
- **안녕? 내 이름은 마이클이야.**     Hi, my name is Michael.
- **안녕? 내 이름은 킴이야.**     Hi, my name is Kim.

**Speak like a native with natural expressions**

**What's your name?** 이름이 뭐야? ◁

**I'm Mary** 난 매리야. ◁
▸ **세윤이야** I am Se-yoon.

**I came from the U.S.** 미국에서 왔어. ◁
[미구게서]
▸ **인도** India
▸ **필리핀** Philippines
▸ **말레이시아** Malaysia

**I'm Australian.** 호주 사람이야. ◁
▸ **캐나다** Canada
▸ **이탈리아** Italy
▸ **나이지리아** Nigeria

**I'm 17.** 17살이야. ◁
[열일곱살]
● Keep in mind that when speaking about age in Korean, we used native numbers.

**Where do you live?** 넌 어디에 살아? ◁
● You might often hear "집이 어디야?", which literally means "where is your house?". Both expressions have similar meanings.

**Nice to meet you.** 반가워. ◁
[방가워]
● '반가워' is a shorter way of saying '만나서 반가워'; however, it is more common to simply use '반가워' in everyday conversation.

145

**How old are you?**

몇 살이야? ◀

[며싸리야]

**What's your hobby?**

취미가 뭐야? ◀

- This can be asked in another way, such as using the question "뭐 좋아해?", which means "what do you like to do?"

**Do you want to eat this?**

이거 좀 먹을래? ◀

- This might sound weird, but a very common way for Koreans to show that they would like to get more familiar with someone and become friends is to share their food, if they have any. So, if there is someone you want to get to know better, try sharing simple snacks like candy or chocolate with them.

Write down the appropriate sentence in the blank space and practice your pronunciations by reading out loud.

**Sooah**   안녕? 내 이름은 수아야. _____ ? ❶
Hi, my name is Sooah. What's your name?

**Robert**   나는 로버트야. 반가워.
I'm Robert. Nice to meet you.

**Sooah**   미국에서 왔어?
Are you from America?

**Robert**   아니, _____ . ❷
No, I'm from Australia.

**Sooah**   응, 지금은 어디에 살아?
I see, where do you live now?

**Robert**   _____ . ❸
I live in Sinchon.

**Answer**

❶ What's your name?    넌 이름이 뭐야?
❷ I'm from Australia.    호주에서 (왔어).
❸ I live in Sinchon.    신촌(에 살아).

TRACK 65

# 두 분 다 건강하십니다.

**My parents are healthy.**

 **Do you want to know How to introduce yourself to your In-laws to be?**

Most people might be curious about communicating with elderly people, especially when introducing oneself to their in-laws. When meeting elders in Korea, it is culturally appropriate for them to do most of the talking and they might ask a lot of questions. Therefore, you need to practice the best and most polite responses. Today's lesson will be on questions that elders ask frequently, and how to answer them.

## Today's Pattern

| N(+은/는) | V+십니다/이십니다. |
|:---:|:---:|
| 두 분 다 | 건강하십니다. |
| **My parents** | **are healthy.** |

**My parents are healthy.**
두 분 다 건강하십니다.

## 5 Key Sentences

- 두 분 다 건강하십니다.     My parents are healthy.
- 부모님은 잘 지내고 계세요.     My parents are doing very well.
- 아버지, 어머니 모두 건강하세요.     Father and Mother are healthy.
- 아버지는 돌아가셨습니다.     Father has passed on.
- 어머니는 몸이 좀 편찮으십니다.     My mother's health is a bit poor.

**Speak like a native with natural expressions**

**It must have taken some trouble to get here.**

**오느라 고생 많았네.** 🔊

▸ **수고했어** to spend a lot of effort

● This is a greeting that elderly people use often when meeting guests who have come from far. You can think of it as a way of saying welcome.

● '고생 많았다' and '수고했다' have very similar meanings and can be used interchangeably.

**How long did it take for you to get here?**

**오는 데 얼마나 걸렸어?** 🔊

● This is another very commonly asked question to find out how much time it took you to get there or what mode of transport you used. It can be used of as an icebreaker.

**How are your parents?**

**부모님은 잘 계세요 ?** 🔊

▸ **건강하세요?** How are your parents' health?

● 계시다 is an honorific word for 있다.

**What do your parents do?**

**부모님은 무슨 일을 하시나?** 🔊

● Asking about the well-being of your parents is an indispensable greeting. After that, they would usually ask about your parents' ages, your parents' jobs, your relationship with them, your current job etc. Be prepared to be asked questions about your family, just as much as questions about your job or plans.

**My father is an architect.**

**아버지는 건축가이십니다 .** 🔊

▸ **사업가이십니다** businessman
▸ **회계사이십니다** accountant
▸ **음식점을 하십니다** runs a restaurant
▸ **농사 지으십니다** farmer

**149**

| | |
|---|---|
| **My mother retired last year.** | 어머니는 작년에 은퇴하셨어요. 🔊 |
| **She is 63 years old this year.** | 올해 63세이십니다. 🔊<br>[육십삼세 or 예순셋] |
| **I have an older sister and two younger brothers.** | <u>언니 한 명</u>이랑 <u>남동생 한 명</u>이 있어요. 🔊 |

> ▶ **형 두 명** two older brothers
> ▶ **여동생 세 명** three younger sisters

| | |
|---|---|
| **I am an international lawyer.** | 저는 <u>국제 변호사</u>입니다. 🔊 |

> ▶ **대사관에서 일하고 있습니다** I work at an embassy
> ▶ **영어 선생님입니다** I am an English teacher

| | |
|---|---|
| **I graduated from the University of Chicago.** | 시카고 대학을 나왔습니다. 🔊 |

> ● Here, '나왔습니다' (coming from the verb 나오다, meaning to come out) means to have graduated from a school (졸업했습니다; 졸업하다).

## Reference

It can be very helpful for you to perceive your first meeting with your in-laws or prospective in-laws as a type of interview. This is because you will have to pay more attention to using honorifics (높임말, literally 'high speech') while speaking. Using honorific endings like '-세요, 이세요, 하세요' comes off as softer and friendlier, while endings such as '-십니다, -이십니다, -하십니다' are more formal and imposing. As each family has its own atmosphere expectations, it is a good idea to speak with your partner and decide which type to use.

Write down the appropriate sentence in the blank space and practice your pronunciations by reading out loud.

**Girlfriend's mother**    **어서 와, 오느라 고생했어.**

Welcome, it must have been difficult to get here.

**Dustin**    **어머님, 안녕하세요?**

Good afternoon, ma'am.

**Girlfriend's mother**    **그래. 편하게 앉아. 부모님은 잘 계시고?**

Great. Please have a seat and make yourself comfortable. How are your parents?

**Dustin**    **네, _____. ❶**

Yes, both my parents are healthy.

**Girlfriend's mother**    **부모님은 무슨 일을 하시나?**

What do your parents do?

**Dustin**    _____ ❷

**그리고** _____ ❸

My father is an architect and my mother is a teacher.

---

**Answer**

❶ Both my parents are healthy.
두 분 다 건강하십니다. or 부모님은 잘 지내고 계세요.
or 아버지, 어머니 모두 건강하세요.

❷ My father is an architect. 아버지는 건축가이십니다.

❸ My mother is a teacher. 어머니는 선생님이십니다.

TRACK 67

# 왜 우리 회사에 지원했나요?
**What made you apply to our company?**

 **Do you want to know How to introduce yourself during a job interview?**

In Korea, in order to qualify for a job interview, you need to at least be able to speak Korean at the intermediate level. Additionally, it is a basic required communication skill needed not only for the interview, but also in carrying out your work duties and to form good interpersonal relationships at work. Today's lesson will cover basic introductions, and frequently asked questions during job interviews. Most of them are very essential questions, so those who are preparing for interviews should practice responses that match their situation.

## Today's **Pattern**

지원 동기

## 왜 우리 회사에 지원했나요?

**Reason for application**

**What made you apply to our company?**
왜 우리 회사에 지원했나요?

### 5 Key Sentences

- 왜 우리 회사에 지원했나요?
- 자기소개 부탁드립니다.
- 마이클 씨의 강점은 무엇인가요?
- 레베카 씨의 약점은 무엇입니까?
- 우리 회사가 엔조 씨를 채용해야 하는 이유를 말해 보세요.

What made you apply to our company?
Please introduce yourself.
Mr. Michael, what are your strengths?
Ms. Rebecca, what are your weaknesses?
Mr. Enzo, please tell us why our company should hire you.

**Speak like a native with natural expressions**

| | |
|---|---|
| **Could you briefly introduce yourself?** | 간단하게 자기소개 해 주시겠어요? |

**Good morning**

안녕하십니까?

- You can also say '안녕하세요?'. However, depending on the company culture or scale, more formal greetings might be more acceptable, so be sure to check any information on this beforehand.

**My name is Chris.**

제 이름은 크리스입니다.

**I majored in video design at New York University.**

뉴욕 대학교에서 영상 디자인을 전공했습니다.

- ▸ **경영학** Management
- ▸ **무역학** International trade
- ▸ **교육학** Education/pedagogy

**Why do you want to work in our company?**

왜 우리 회사에서 일하고 싶으세요?

- This question asks about your reason for applying to that company. This is an important question, so prepare and practice your answer ahead of time.

**Did you make any special efforts to join our company?**

우리 회사에 들어오기 위해 특별히 노력한 것이 있나요?

- This question is asked to determine how serious the candidate is.

**What are your strengths, Ms. Sara?**

사라 씨의 강점은 무엇입니까?

- ▸ **약점** weaknesses

**153**

**What would you do if you disagree with your superior when you work?**

일할 때 <u>상사와</u> 의견이 다르면 어떻게 하시겠어요? 🔊

▷ **팀원과** with team members

- This is to examine the applicant's attitude towards problems that arise due to interpersonal relationships, and how they might resolve them.

**What do you think is the most important thing in life?**

인생에서 가장 중요한 것이 무엇이라고 생각하시나요? 🔊

- This is a question about the candidate's values.

**Tell us about someone you respect.**

존경하는 사람에 대해서 말해 보세요. 🔊

- You should prepare your answer about a person you respect and why you respect them.

Write down the appropriate sentence in the blank space and practice your pronunciations by reading out loud.

**Interviewer** 반갑습니다. 간단하게 자기소개 부탁드릴게요.

Nice to meet you. Please introduce yourself.

**Dustin** _____ . ❶ 미국에서 영상 디자인을 전공했고, 이번에 콘텐츠 개발팀에 지원했습니다.

Hello, my name is Dustin. I majored in video design in the U.S., and I have applied to work in the content development team.

**Interviewer** 알겠습니다, _____? ❷

Okay, what made you apply to our company?

**Dustin** 알파 코리안 클래스의 유튜브 채널의 애청자로서 채널 기획에 직접 참여하고 싶었기 때문입니다.

As a fan of the Alpha Korean class Youtube channel, I want to directly participate in the planning of the channel.

**Interviewer** 좋습니다, _____? ❸

Good. Then, what are your strengths?

**Dustin** 저는 재학 시절 만든 광고 영상으로 2개의 공모전에 입상한 경험이 있습니다. 그래서 짧은 시간에 사람들의 이목을 사로잡는 스토리텔링에 자신이 있습니다.

I won two contests in creating advertisement videos when I was in school. Therefore, I am confident in my ability in story-telling, which can capture people's attention instantly.

**Answer**

❶ Hello, my name is James.
안녕하십니까, 제 이름은 더스틴입니다. or 안녕하세요, 제 이름은 더스틴입니다.

❷ What made you apply to our company?
왜 우리 회사에 지원했나요? or 왜 우리 회사에서 일하고 싶으세요?

❸ What are your strengths? 더스틴 씨의 강점은 무엇인가요?

TRACK 69

# 카톡 아이디 좀 알려 줄래요?
## Can I have your Kakao ID?

 **Do you want to know How to ask for someone's contact information?**

Would you like to become friends with the people you like in Korea? Perhaps, you would like to have conversations over coffee or go out for a movie with them? Or you may want to go to good restaurants for a meal or two, or have a good time with them at the karaoke bar. In order to become friends and do all the fun activities with them, you must firstly take the initiative and get their contact information. Today, we will go over some expressions that you need when making friends.

### Today's **Pattern**

| N | 좀 알려 줄래요? |
|---|---|
| **카톡 아이디** | **좀 알려 줄래요?** |
| **Kakaotalk ID** | **Can I have** |

**Can I have your Kakao ID?**
카톡 아이디 좀 알려 줄래요?

### 5 Key Sentences

- **카톡 아이디 좀 알려 줄래요?**    Can I have your Kakao ID?
- **전화번호 좀 알려 줄래요?**    Can I have your phone number?
- **이메일 주소 좀 알려 줄래요?**    Can I have your email address?
- **인스타그램 아이디 좀 알려 줄래요?**    Can I have your Instagram ID?
- **페이스북 아이디 좀 알려 줄래요?**    Can I have your Facebook ID?

**Speak like a native with natural expressions**

| | |
|---|---|
| Do you have Kakao Talk ID? | 카톡 아이디 있어요? 🔊 |

May I ask your age?

나이가 어떻게 되세요? 🔊

▸ **성함이** Name (formal)
[성아미]

● '나이가 어떻게 되세요?' is used to ask for age, just like the expression '몇 살이세요?'. However, it is a softer, more indirect way to ask. '성함이 어떻게 되세요?' is also used to ask for someone's name, just like '이름이 뭐예요?', but it is more polite and formal.

How can I contact you later?

나중에 어떻게 연락할 수 있을까요? 🔊

I just sent you a message on Kakaotalk.

지금 카톡으로 메세지 보냈어요. 🔊

Do you do Instagram?

인스타 해요? 🔊

▸ **페북** Facebook
▸ **트위터** Twitter

● Facebook(페이스북) called 페북 for short.

Let's follow each other.

우리 맞팔해요. 🔊

● Following each other on SNS is called '맞팔하다'. It's a newly coined word.

Let's become friends.

우리 친구 해요. 🔊

▸ **인친** instagram friend

Let's be friends from now on.

우리 앞으로 친하게 지내요. 🔊

● Say this if you meet someone who you want to get along with really well.

**Just call me unni**

**그냥 언니라고 불러요.** 🔊

> ▸ **형이라고** Hyung (elder brother)

- The first step to become closer is to change the way you address the other person. If the other party is older and asks you to call them 언니, 오빠 or 형, it means that they would like to become closer to you

**You can speak casually with me.**

**저한테 말 놓으세요.** 🔊

> ▸ **편하게 하세요** Speak comfortably to me.

- Both '말을 놓다' and '말을 편하게 하다' are expressions to let others know that they can speak to you without honorifics, that is, using 반말. The expression '반말하세요' (speak in banmal to me) is not used as often.

- You can say this to people Older than you whom you like; it could make you become closer faster.

**Let's grab a drink soon.**

**조만간 술 한잔해요.** 🔊

> ▸ **다음에** next time

## Reference

Kakaotalk (카카오톡) is often shortened to 카톡. It is a messenger app similar to Whatsapp that almost all Koreans use. If you share your Kakaotalk ID, making Korean friends will become much easier.

Write down the appropriate sentence in the blank space and practice your pronunciations by reading out loud.

Robert      _____? ❶

May I ask your age?

**Seohyeon**    **저는 27살이에요. 그쪽은요?**

I'm 27 years old. What about you?

Robert      **저는 23살이에요.** _____. ❷

I'm 23 years old. Please speak comfortably to me.

**Seohyeon**    **그럴까? 그럼, 너도 그냥 누나라고 불러.**

Shall we? Then, you can just call me noona.

Robert      **네, 누나. 앞으로 친하게 지내요.**

Okay, noona. Let's be friends from now on.

**Seohyeon**    **그래,** _____? ❸

Great, what's your Kakaotalk ID?

### Answer

❶ May I ask your age?      나이가 어떻게 되세요?
❷ Speak comfortably to me.    저한테 말 편하게 하세요.
❸ What's your Kakaotalk ID?    카톡 아이디가 뭐야?

**159**

TRACK 71

# 제 고등학교 친구예요.
## He is my friend from high school.

  **Do you want to know How to introduce your friends?**

One of my students is a former exchange student in Korea. About a month before her program ended, she decided to travel around Korea with her parents and friends from the US. Upon reaching Korea, she introduced her parents and friends to others so that everyone got the opportunity to get to know each other. In to-day's lesson, we will practice how to introduce your family and friends to other people.

### Today's Pattern

| 제 | N+친구 | 예요. |
|---|---|---|
| **제** | **고등학교 친구** | **예요.** |
| My | a friend from high school | He is |

**He is my friend from high school.**
제 ~친구예요.

- This expression describes a friend whom you went to high school with. Most times in everyday conversation, people shorten it to 'school/group name + 친구예요'.

### 5 Key  Sentences

- 제 고등학교 친구예요.   He is my friend from high school.
- 제 중학교 친구예요.   He's my friend from middle school.
- 제 초등학교 친구예요.   He's my friend from elementary school.
- 제 대학교 친구예요.   He's my college friend.
- 제 직장 동료예요.   He is my co-worker.

**Speak like a native with natural expressions** 🎧

| | |
|---|---|
| **Let me introduce my best friend.** | 제 단짝 친구를 소개할게요. 🔊 |

▸ **베프** best friend
● The word '베프' is short for 'best friend', and is commonly used among younger people.

| | |
|---|---|
| **This is my closest friend, Isabella.** | 이쪽은 저랑 제일 친한 친구 이사벨이에요. 🔊 |

| | |
|---|---|
| **She is one year older than I am.** | 저보다 한 살 많아요. 🔊 |

▸ **어려요** younger

| | |
|---|---|
| **He was my roommate from college.** | 대학 때 룸메이트였어요. 🔊 |

| | |
|---|---|
| **We have been friends since elementary school.** | 초등학교 때부터 친했어요. 🔊 |

● When introducing a friend you have known for a long time, using the pattern '~때부터' sounds more natural.

| | |
|---|---|
| **I met her at a book club.** | 독서 모임에서 만났어요. 🔊 |

▸ **테니스 클럽** tennis club

| | |
|---|---|
| **Eric works for Google** | 에릭은 구글에서 일해요. 🔊 |

▸ **국제학교** international school

| | |
|---|---|
| **Jonathan is a singer** | 조나단은 가수예요. 🔊 |

▸ **배우예요** actor
▸ **앱 개발자예요** app developer
▸ **의대생이에요** medical school student

**She has been good at computers since she was young.**

어렸을 때부터 컴퓨터를 잘했어요. 🔊

▸ **노래를 좋아했어요** good at singing
▸ **인기가 많았어요** been popular

**This is my mother. Her name is Ann**

이분이 제 어머니세요. 성함은 앤이에요. 🔊

▸ **아버지** father

**My parents cannot speak Korean.**

제 부모님은 한국어를 못해요. 🔊

Write down the appropriate sentence in the blank space and practice your pronunciations by reading out loud.

Mary      선생님. 제 친구를 소개할게요. _____. ❶

Ma'am, let me introduce my friend. This is my best friend, Matthew.

Helena ssam      반가워요. 저는 매리의 선생님이에요.

Nice to meet you. I'm Mary's teacher.

Mary      _____. ❷

Matthew doesn't speak Korean.

Helena ssam      아, 그렇구나. 매튜 씨도 학생이에요?

Oh, I see. Is he a student, too?

Mary      아니요, _____. ❸
어렸을 때부터 인기가 많았어요.

No, Matthew is an actor. He has been popular since childhood.

Helena ssam      우와, 진짜 멋져요. !

Wow, that's awesome!

**Answer**

❶ This is my best friend, Matthew.      이쪽은 저랑 제일 친한 친구 매튜예요.
❷ Matthew doesn't speak Korean.      매튜는 한국어를 못해요.
❸ Matthew is a movie star.      매튜는 배우예요.

# UNIT 7

# Expressing yourself

TRACK 73

# 이건 아니야.
## This is not right!

 ## Do you want to know Korean exclamations?

In Korean language, there are several short exclamations that are most suitable to use in certain situations. These words can accurately express one's emotions or thoughts better than any long and wordy sentence. Exclamations (감탄사) are short and easy to memorize, therefore once you are familiarized with these exclamations, you can use them with ease. Of course, it is important to know the right time and situation to use them for. This lesson will cover these exclamations that are most frequently used.

### Today's **Pattern**

#### Exclamations
## 이건 아니야.

Something you can say when you think something wrong is happening, or when you're angry. There are also many words that have been transformed into "이건 아니지."or "이건 좀 아니지 않나요?"

**This is not right! (This is wrong)**
### 이건 아니야. or 이건 아니지.

### 5 Key Sentences

- **이건 아니야.**    This is not right!
- **우와!**    Wow!
- **대박!**    Amazing!
- **최고!**    Fantastic!
- **진짜?**    Really?

**Speak like a native with natural expressions**

**That's right.**

맞아요. 🔈

- Many times, when someone thinks that what their partner has said is right, they say '맞아, 맞아' several times to show their agreement.

**Of course. That's what I'm saying.**

그럼요. 🔈

▸ 그러니까요
▸ 그니까요.

- The expressions '내 말이' means that both speakers agree on what is being discussed. It is used when both parties feel the same way about something.

**Ah!**

아! 🔈

- Exclamations such as '아!', '아하!' or '오호' are used before saying that you understand something.

**Oh my!**

아이고! 🔈

- This exclamation can be used in any situation, whether you are surprised, hurt, having a hard time, or meeting someone you haven't seen in a while.

**No way!**

말도 안 돼! 🔈

- This is an exclamation you say to yourself when facing something that sounds over exaggerated, mysterious or completely absurd.

**Oh my goodness!**

헐! 🔈

- Just like 'Oh my goodness!', this can be used in various situations.

**Gosh!**

어머! 📢

- This is often used by women when they are surprised.

**That's crazy!**

미쳤다! 📢

- This is another expression that can be used when you are surprised. It can also be used in several modified forms, such as '미쳤어', '미친 거 아니야?' and '미쳤네'.

**Hmph!**

흥! 📢

- This expression is used when the other person has done something upsetting, or when you are sulking, but it has a cute nuance to it. 흥, 칫 and 뿡 are often used together like a set of three.

**What should I do?!**

어떡해! 📢

- This is a shortened form of '어떻게 해'. This is used in awkward situations when you are not sure what to do.

Write down the appropriate sentence in the blank space and practice your pronunciations by reading out loud.

---

**Seohyeon**    _____ ❶, 펜타포트 락 페스티벌 취소됐다며.

What should we do?! I heard the Pentaport Rock Festival has been canceled.

**Minjun**    뭐? 누가 그래?

What? Who said that?

**Seohyeon**    뉴스에서 그러던데? 호우 경보 때문에.

I heard it on the news. It's because of the heavy rain warning.

**Minjun**    _____ ? ❷

Gosh~ Really?

**Seohyeon**    이거 봐 봐. 맞지?

Look at this. Right?

**Minjun**    _____ ! ❸

No way! This isn't right.

**Answer**

❶ What should I do?        어떡해?
❷ Gosh~ Really?        헐, 진짜?
❸ No way! This isn't right!    안 돼. 이건 아니야.

TRACK 75

# 이걸 한국어로 어떻게 말해요?
## How do I say this in Korean?

 **Do you want to know** How to ask for the meaning of something in Korean?

Most of the time, we remember words we learn from everyday conversations rather than from reading books or language classes, Wouldn't it be great to learn Korean by asking questions you are curious about whenever you have the chance? You can even ask questions about cultural nuances that you don't understand or casual words used among friends and family. Today, we will learn how to ask about the Korean language and culture using different expressions.

## Today's Pattern

| N(+을/를) | 한국어로 | 어떻게 말해요? |
|---|---|---|
| **이걸** | **한국어로** | **어떻게 말해요?** |
| This | in Korean | How do I say |

**Can I get the Tteokbokki and Sundae?**
~랑/이랑 ~주세요.

## 5 Key Sentences

- **이걸 한국어로 어떻게 말해요?**　　How do I say this in Korean?
- **Coin을 한국어로 어떻게 말해요?**　　How do I say 'coin' in Korean?
- **Card를 한국어로 어떻게 말해요?**　　How do I say 'card' in Korean?
- **Water를 한국어로 어떻게 말해요?**　　How do I say 'water' in Korean?
- **Grandma를 한국어로 어떻게 말해요?**　　How do I say 'grandma' in Korean?

**Speak like a native with natural expressions**

**How do I say this in Korean?**

이게 한국어로 뭐예요? 🔊
[항구거로]

**How do you say 'I really like your dress' in Korean?**

'I really like your dress'는 한국어로 뭐라고 해요? 🔊

**What does that mean?**

그게 무슨 뜻이에요? 🔊

▸ **의미예요**

● 뜻=의미 meaning
● When having a conversation in Korean and you come across a word that you don't know, you can ask for its meaning by using this sentence pattern.

**How do you use this in a sentence?**

이걸 문장으로 어떻게 말해요? 🔊

**Does this expression sound natural?**

이 표현이 자연스러운가요? 🔊

● Are you worried that an expression is grammatically correct, but sounds awkward because it is not often used by native speakers? Then you can ask this question.

**Please tell me if this is right.**

이게 맞는지 한번 봐 주세요. 🔊

● The expression '한번 봐 주세요' is often used together with the pattern 'V+ㄴ/인지'. 'V+ㄴ/인지' is connective ending used when speaking about events or thoughts that you are unsure of.

**Please translate this sentence into Korean for me.**

이 문장을 한국어로 번역해 주세요. 🔊

**That word is an abbreviation.**　　그 말은 <u>줄임말</u>이에요. 🔊

> **은어**예요 jargon, slang
> **비속어**예요 swear word
> **유행어**예요 buzzword
> **신조어**예요 newly coined word

**I don't know how to say it in Korean.**　　한국어로 어떻게 말하는지 모르겠어요. 🔊

**Is it rude to say this?**　　이렇게 말하면 무례한가요? 🔊

Write down the appropriate sentence in the blank space and practice your pronunciations by reading out loud.

**Dustin** _____? ❶

How do you say "Policeman" in Korean?

**Helena ssam** '경찰'이라고 해요.

It's called '경찰'.

**Dustin** 그럼, _____? ❷

So, what does 'japsae' (various birds) mean?

**Helena ssam** 네? 잡새요?

What? 'japsae'?

**Dustin** 짭새! 짭새요.

Jjapsae! It's Jjapsae.

**Helena ssam** 아, _____. ❸ 경찰이라는 뜻이에요.

Oh, that's a slang word. It means police.

TRACK 77

# 제 고향은 나이지리아입니다.
## I am from Nigeria.

 **Do you want to know How to talk about your background?**

Where is your hometown? What is that region known for? What kind of student were you during your schooling days? When you meet someone new or a new group of people, you are likely to get asked such questions during a conversation. You may also be asking the same questions in return. It is a way of getting to know each other better and forming new friendships with others. This lesson will be about expressions you will need to know and use when talking about your background.

---

**Today's Pattern**

| 제 고향은 | N+입니다. |
|---|---|
| **제 고향은** | **나이지리아입니다.** |
| **My hometown** | **is Nigeria.** |

**I am from Nigeria.**
제 고향은 ~입니다.

---

**5 Key** **Sentences**

- 제 고향은 나이지리아입니다.    I am from Nigeria.
- 제 고향은 포르투갈입니다.    I am from Portugal.
- 제 고향은 서울입니다.    My hometown is Seoul.
- 제 고향은 시드니입니다.    My hometown is Sydney.
- 제 고향은 런던입니다.    My hometown is London.

**Speak like a native with natural expressions**

**Where is your hometown?**

고향이 어디예요? ◁
[고양이]

**Seoul is the capital city of South Korea.**

서울은 대한민국의 수도입니다. ◁

**Busan is the second largest city in South Korea.**

부산은 한국에서 두 번째로 큰 도시입니다. ◁

**Suncheon is a medium-sized city in the Southern region.**

순천은 남부 지방의 중소 도시입니다. ◁

▸ 중부 centre; central region
▸ 동부 cast; castern region
▸ 서부 west; western region
▸ 북부 north; northern region

● When talking about regions, the cardinal directions 동, 서, 남, 북 are used: they correspond to east, west, south and north respectively. North west is '북서부', and south east is '남동부'. The 부 (Hanja: 部) used here is from the hanja for 'region'.

● Usually, cities with a population of at least 500,000 are called large cities (대도시), while those with less than 200,000 are called small cities (소도시). In between those two figures, there are medium-sized cities, called 중소 도시.

**Jeonju is famous for bibimbap.**

전주는 비빔밥으로 유명합니다.
[비빔빠브로]

**The Busan International Film Festival takes place every year.**

매년 부산 국제 영화제가 열려요.

**I graduated from a public high school**

저는 공립 고등학교를 나왔습니다.

▸ **사립** private

**My middle school was a co-ed school.**

우리 중학교는 <u>남녀공학</u>이었어요.

▸ **여중/여고** girls-only
▸ **남중/남고** boys-only

**I was a very quiet child.**

저는 매우 <u>조용한</u> 아이였어요.

▸ **반항적인** rebellious
▸ **활발한** lively, outgoing
▸ **장난기 많은** mischievous
▸ **조숙한** precocious

**When I was younger, I spent a lot of time at the beach.**

어렸을 때는 <u>바닷가에서</u> 많은 시간을 보냈어요.

▸ **도서관에서** at the library
▸ **놀이터에서** at the playground

Write down the appropriate sentence in the blank space and practice your pronunciations by reading out loud.

**Sooah**   로버트 씨는 고향이 어디예요?

Where is your hometown, Robert?

**Robert**   _____ . ❶

It's Sussex in England.

**Sooah**   서식스는 어디에 있어요?

Where's Sussex?

**Robert**   _____ . ❷

It's in southeastern England.

**Sooah**   그곳은 뭘로 유명해요?

What is it famous for?

**Robert**   _____ . ❸ 영국에서 가장 큰 예술 축제예요.

The Brighton Festival is held every year. It is the biggest art festival in England.

---

**Answer**

❶ It's Sussex in England.        영국 서식스예요.
❷ It's in southeastern England.   영국 남동부에 있어요.
❸ The Brighton Festival is held every year.   매년 브라이튼 페스티벌이 열려요.

TRACK 79

# 저는 회계사예요.
## I'm an accountant.

 **Do you want to know How to talk about your job?**

It is quite common for Koreans to ask when they meet you for the first time: "what do you do for work?"; '무슨 일을 하세요?' This is probably because most Koreans have the perception that what someone does for a living says a lot about who they are. You need to learn to answer this question, as you can expect to get it quite often. Let's learn and practice how to talk about your job in today's lesson.

### Today's **Pattern**

| 저는 | N+예요/이에요. |
|---|---|
| **저는** | **회계사예요.** |
| **I'm** | **an accountant.** |

**I'm an accountant.**
저는 ~예요/이에요.

### 5 Key Sentences

- 저는 회계사예요.     I'm an accountant.
- 저는 의사예요.     I'm a doctor.
- 저는 영어 선생님이에요.     I'm an English teacher.
- 저는 사진 작가예요.     I'm a photographer.
- 저는 그래픽 디자이너예요.     I'm a graphic designer.

**Speak like a native with natural expressions**

**What do you do for a living?** 무슨 일 하세요?

▸ **어떤 일** what kind of work

● This is one of the most common questions used when asking about someone's job.

**Where is your workplace?** 직장이 어디에 있어요?

**Where do you work?** 어디에 다녀요?

● The expression '-에 다니다' is used to describe a place that you regularly go, such as where you go to for work or the school you attend. It is often used to ask what company you work for.

**I work in a publishing company.** 출판사에 다녀요.

▸ **병원에** hospital
▸ **법원에** law firm
▸ **화장품 회사** cosmetics company
▸ **요리 학원** culinary school

**What do you do there?** 거기서 무슨 일 하세요?

● This is a question asked to find out specifically about someone's job responsibilities at work. It asks for more details such as the department one works at, or the actual tasks or position in the company.

**I am the team manager in the sales department.** 저는 영업부 팀장입니다.

▸ **인사부 대리** assistant manager of personnel department
▸ **사장/ 대표** president/CEO
▸ **개발팀 연구원** development team researcher

**179**

**I work in the fashion industry.**　패션 업계에서 일해요. 🔊

- ▶ **제조** manufacturing
- ▶ **미용** beauty
- ▶ **교육** education
- ● Using this expression allows you to talk about a wider occupational field.

**I work as a freelance writer**　프리랜서 작가로 일하고 있어요. 🔊

- ▶ **헤어 스타일리스트로** Hairstylist
- ▶ **관광 가이드로** tourist guide
- ▶ **메이크업 아티스트로** makeup artist
- ▶ **스킨케어 컨설턴트로** skin care consultant

**I make coffee in a cafe.**　카페에서 커피를 만들어요. 🔊

- ▶ **베이커리에서 빵을** bread at a bakery
- ● By describing your actual duties at the workplace, you can explain about your job in more detail.

**I am filming a movie.**　저는 영화를 찍고 있어요. 🔊

- ▶ **신발을 만들고** making shoes
- ▶ **책을 쓰고** writing a book

Write down the appropriate sentence in the blank space and practice your pronunciations by reading out loud.

**Siwoo** 제니퍼 씨는 무슨 일 하세요?

Jennifer, what do you do for a living?

**Jennifer** _____. ❶

I work at a publishing company.

**Siwoo** 네, 거기서 무슨 일 하세요?

Oh, what do you do there?

**Jennifer** _____. ❷

I publish books.

**Siwoo** 그럼, 편집자세요?

So, are you an editor?

**Jennifer** 아니요. _____. ❸

No, I'm a CEO.

TRACK 81

# 저는 3남매 중 첫째예요.
**I am the eldest of 3 siblings.**

  **Do you want to know How to talk about your family?**

In Korean culture, a family is perceived as something very important in a person's life. Family is not limited to the immediate family (i.e. partner and kids), but it includes parents and siblings as well. This stems from a common belief that a person's family background has much influence on his/her personality. Today, let's practice how to talk about your family.

---

### Today's **Pattern**

| 저는 | N 중 | N+예요/이에요. |
|------|------|----------------|
| **저는** | **3남매 중** | **첫째예요.** |
| I | of 3 siblings | am the eldest |

**I am the eldest of 3 siblings.**
저는 ~예요/이에요.

---

### 5 Key Sentences

- 저는 3남매 중 첫째예요.      I am the eldest of 3 siblings.
- 저는 5형제 중 막내예요.      I am the youngest of 5 siblings.
- 저는 8남매 중 셋째예요.      I am the third child of 8 siblings.
- 저는 외동이에요.           I am an only child.
- 저는 쌍둥이에요.           I have a twin.

- 남매 means children born to same parents. 형제 is a word that can refer to both brothers or siblings of both genders.

**Speak like a native with natural expressions**

| | |
|---|---|
| My family is made up of 5 people. | 우리 가족은 모두 5명이에요. ◁<br>[다섯명] |
| There is me, my parents and my two older brothers. | 저랑 부모님 그리고 오빠 두 명이 있어요. ◁ |
| I have two younger sisters. | 저는 여동생만 두 명이 있어요. ◁ |
| My family lives with my grandparents. | 우리 가족은 조부모님과 같이 살아요. ◁<br>▸ **고양이 2마리와** with two cats<br>▸ **개 한 마리와** with one dog |
| I have no siblings since I am an only child. | 저는 외동이라서 형제가 없어요. ◁<br>▸ **외동딸** Only daughter<br>▸ **외동아들** Only son |
| My mother passed away when I was young. | 어머니는 어렸을 때 돌아가셨어요. ◁ |
| My parents got divorced, so I live with my mom now. | 부모님이 이혼을 하셔서 저는 엄마랑 살았어요. ◁<br>▸ **아빠하고 새엄마랑** father and step-mother<br>● The word for 'stepmother' in Korean is '새엄마', while the word for 'stepfather' is '새아빠'. |

**183**

**Everyone in my family like to go fishing.**

우리 가족은 모두 <u>낚시를</u> 좋아해요. ◁ᴗ

▹ **보드게임을** board games
▹ **한국 드라마를** Korean dramas

**There is a big age gap between me and my younger siblings.**

동생들이랑 저는 <u>나이 차이가</u> 많이 나요. ◁ᴗ

▹ **1살 차이가** one-year apart

**My older brother and I do not have anything in common.**

형과 저는 공통점이 없어요. ◁ᴗ

▹ **공통점이 많아요** have a lot in common.

Write down the appropriate sentence in the blank space and practice your pronunciations by reading out loud.

| | |
|---|---|
| **Seohyeon** | **로버트 씨는 외동이에요?**<br>Are you an only child? |
| **Robert** | **아니요?** _____. ❶<br>No, I'm the eldest of three siblings. |
| **Seohyeon** | **진짜요? 장남은 아닌 것 같았는데.**<br>Really? I didn't think of you as the eldest child. |
| **Robert** | **그래요?** _____. ❷<br>Really? There's a big age difference between me and my younger siblings. |
| **Seohyeon** | **동생들이랑 친해요?**<br>Are you close to your siblings? |
| **Robert** | **서로** _____. ❸ **그래서 별로 안 친해요.**<br>We don't have anything in common. So, we're not that close. |

### Answer

❶ I'm the eldest of three siblings.　　저는 3남매 중 장남이에요.

❷ There's a big age difference between me and my younger siblings.
동생들이랑 저는 나이 차이가 많이 나요.

❸ We don't have anything in common.　　서로 공통점이 없어요.

TRACK 83

# 죄송하지만 괜찮습니다.

**Sorry. I am not interested.**

 **Do you want to know** How to respectfully express your dislikes?

In daily interactions with others, there will be times when you must refuse what is offered, either because you don't like it, or prefer something else. At such times, if you openly say '싫어요' ('I don't like it') or '아니에요' ('No') you may appear to be rude and unintentionally create an awkward atmosphere. To prevent such situations, let's look at how to respectfully reject things in a way that is less hurtful. In this lesson, you will learn the simple rule of first saying thank you or sorry, and then giving your reason for refusing.

## Today's Pattern

| 죄송하지만 | 괜찮습니다(or reason for rejection) |
|---|---|
| **죄송하지만** | **괜찮습니다.** |
| **I'm sorry but** | **I am not interested.** |

**Sorry, I am not interested.**
죄송하지만 ~ㅂ/습니다.

## 5 Key Sentences

- **죄송하지만 괜찮습니다.**          Sorry, I am not interested.
- **죄송하지만 시간이 없습니다.**     Sorry, but I don't have time.
- **죄송하지만 돈이 없습니다.**       Sorry, I don't have any money.
- **죄송하지만 약속이 있습니다.**     Sorry, but I have a prior engagement..
- **죄송하지만 할 수 없습니다.**      Sorry, but I can't do that.

**Speak like a native with natural expressions**

**I'm good. I am full right now.**

괜찮아요. 이제 배불러요. ◁

- This expression is used much more often than '싫어요' and '안 돼요' when respectfully turning something down. You can say '괜찮아' when someone offers you something you find difficult to eat, or when you are full and can't eat anymore.

**I'll think about it more.**

좀 더 생각해 보겠습니다. ◁

- When you have been asked a question that is difficult to answer at the moment, use this expression to buy more time.

**Thank you, but I don't think I will be able to go.**

고맙지만 갈 수 없을 것 같아요. ◁
[갈쑤업쓸꺼까타요]

▷ **할** to do
▷ **기다릴** to wait

- The expression '~을 수 없을 것 같아요' (meaning 'I don't think I'll be able to) is another way to say that you cannot do something ('할 수 없다'). However, in everyday conversation, it is often used as softer, more indirect rejection than stronger ones like 'I don't want to' ('하고 싶지 않아요').

**It is difficult for me to do that at the moment.**

지금은 조금 곤란해요. ◁
[골라내요]

▷ **어려워요** difficult

- Use this expression when you are currently busy, or for some other reason cannot do someone a favour.

**187**

**Now is not the right time, so let's talk about it later.**　지금은 힘들고, 다음에 다시 얘기해요. 🔊

**I already have a plan for that day.**　그날은 이미 선약이 있어서요. 🔊

**I don't think I am ready yet.**　저는 아직 준비가 안 된 것 같아요. 🔊

**I don't know much about it.**　그건 제가 잘 모르는 분야라서요. 🔊

- This expression is used when you are refusing because you are not the right person to do that.

**That's good too, but I like this item more.**　그것도 좋지만 저는 이게 더 마음에 들어요. 🔊

- This is a polite yet honest way to say that you don't like a recommendation given to you more than another item.

**I really don't want to go right now.**　지금은 정말 가고 싶지 않아요. 🔊

▸ **하고** do
▸ **먹고** eat

- Sometimes, the other party might not understand your polite refusal and keep asking. When that happens, you might need to be straightforward with your refusal. In English, this expression means 'I am really not in the mood'.

Write down the appropriate sentence in the blank space and practice your pronunciations by reading out loud.

**Sooah**  저한테 영화 티켓이 생겼는데, 주말에 같이 볼래요?

I have two movie tickets. Do you want to watch it together on the weekend?

**Minjun**  _____. ❶

Thank you, but I don't think I can go.

**Sooah**  왜요? 주말에도 일해요?

Why? Do you work on weekends?

**Minjun**  아니요. _____. ❷

No, I already have plans on that day.

**Sooah**  누구랑요? 여자 친구랑? 이 티켓 드릴까요?

With whom? With your girlfriend? Would you like to have these tickets?

**Minjun**  _____. ❸

Thank you but I'm not interested.

---

**Answer**

❶ Thank you, but I don't think I can go.    고맙지만 갈 수 없을 것 같아요.

❷ I already have a previous engagement on that day.
그날은 이미 선약이 있어서요.

❸ Thank you but I'm not interested.    괜찮습니다.

TRACK 85

# 시간 될 때 같이 밥 한번 먹어요.

**Let's get some food together when you have time.**

 **Do you want to know How to politely tell someone you are interested in them?**

In life, you might meet an amazing person when you least expected it. Of course, you could end up meeting that special someone who would turn your life around while in Korea (하하). Imagine yourself in that exact moment and ask yourself: how can I express my interest in him/her? If you are interested with someone, one of the most important things for you to do is to get his/her phone number and go on a date. You might be wondering how to achieve all these with that special person. Well, that's exactly what I'll be teaching you today!

## Today's Pattern

| 시간 될 때 같이 | N+먹어요/해요. |
|---|---|
| **시간 될 때 같이** | **밥 한번 먹어요.** |
| **when you have time** | **Let's get some food** |

**Let's get some food together when you have time.**
시간 될 때 같이 N 한번 V+아/어요.

## 5 Key Sentences

- 시간 될 때 같이 밥 한번 먹어요. — Let's get some food together when you have time.
- 시간 될 때 같이 차 한 잔 해요. — When you have time, let's get a cup of tea together.
- 시간 될 때 같이 커피 한 잔 해요. — Let's get some coffee together when you are free.
- 시간 될 때 같이 저녁 한번 먹어요. — Let's have dinner together when you have time.
- 시간 될 때 같이 와인 한 잔 해요. — Let's have some wine together when you have time.

**Speak like a native with natural expressions**

**By any chance, do you have a boyfriend?**

혹시 남자 친구 있으세요? 🔊

▸ **여자 친구** Girlfriend

- Sometimes, it is best to just ask straightforwardly. Adding the adverb '혹시' makes such questions seem less pointed, so that it doesn't sound rude. If there is someone you would like to date, ask like this.

**Would you like to go out with me?**

저랑 한번 만나 보지 않을래요? 🔊

- The expression '사귀어 보자', meaning 'let's try dating' is a more roundabout way of asking someone out. If asked with sincerity, it seems much cooler than just saying '사귀자' ('let's date').

**Excuse me, may I have your number?**

실례지만, 연락처 좀 알 수 있을까요? 🔊

- The expression '알 수 있을까요?' is more indirect than '알려 줄래요?' so it feels softer.

**Would you like to have lunch with me today?**

오늘 점심 같이 먹을래요? 🔊

▸ **내일** tomorrow

**What do you do on the weekends?**

주말에 뭐 하세요? 🔊

- This is a common question, but if you want to make plans to meet him/her outside, you can start by asking this question.

**191**

**Do you want to go see a movie with me?**

저랑 같이 영화 볼래요? 🔊

▶ **넷플릭스 볼래요?** Do you want to watch Netflix?

▶ **등산 갈래요?** Do you want to go hiking?

● When proposing a date, '같이 영화 볼래요?' is probably one of the most common expressions used. It is asking if they want to go the **cinema** (극장) and see a movie with you.

**I will see you to the subway station.**

제가 지하철역까지 바래다 드릴게요. 🔊

▶ **집까지** to (your) house

● After an enjoyable date, Korean men will usually escort their dates back to their houses or at least to the subway station.

**I would like to ask you out on a date.**

데이트 신청하고 싶어요. 🔊

● Because this expression is straightforward, it shows how confident and brave you are.

**Let me know when you get home.**

도착하면 연락 주세요.

● This expression is used to make sure your date gets home safely. It could also be a way to express that you are sad the date is over, and want to talk with them so more!

**Do you want to go out with me?**

우리 사귈래요?

● When both parties are sure that they are interested in each other, asking like this is a good idea, isn't it? Saying this to someone you have just met could seem very rude, so only ask if you have been on at least one date with them.

## Speak with me

Write down the appropriate sentence in the blank space and practice your pronunciations by reading out loud.

---

**Seohyeon**   이름이 뭐예요?
What's your name?

**Robert**   저는 로버트예요. 그쪽은요?
I'm Robert. What about you?

**Seohyeon**   서현이에요. _____ ? ❶
I'm Seohyeon. Do you have a girlfriend?

**Robert**   아니요. 왜요?
No. Why?

**Seohyeon**   _____ . ❷ 주말에 _____ ? ❸
I'd like to ask you out. Would you like to watch a movie with me this weekend?

---

**Robert**   좋아요!
Sure!

**Answer**

❶ Do you have a girlfriend?          혹시 여자 친구 있으세요?
❷ I'd like to ask you out.          데이트 신청하고 싶어서요.
❸ Would you like to watch a movie with me?   저랑 같이 영화 볼래요?

# UNIT 8

# Everyday life

TRACK 87

# 날씨가 후덥지근해요.
## It's hot and humid.

 **Do you want to know How to talk about the weather?**

The weather is the classic go-to conversation starter if you need making a small-talk, especially if you're with a stranger and can't think of anything much to say. In Korea, there are distinct seasons, which means there are many different expressions that can be used to talk about the weather. In the summer, the weather is very hot and humid due to the high atmospheric pressure from the north Pacific Ocean. This climate is called '후덥지근하다', which means 'muggy' or 'humid'. On the other hand, in the winter, the weather becomes dry and cold because of the high air pressure from Siberia. In this lesson, let's take a look at the expressions used to describe the different types of weather in Korea.

### Today's Pattern

| 날씨가 | Adj+아/어요. |
|---|---|
| **날씨가** | **후덥지근해요.** |
| weather | is hot and humid. |

**It's hot and humid.**
날씨가 Adj+아/어요.

### 5 Key Sentences

- **날씨가 후덥지근해요.**     It's hot and humid.
- **날씨가 엄청 더워요.**     It is really hot.
- **날씨가 엄청 추워요.**     The weather is really cold.
- **날씨가 화창해요.**     It is sunny.
- **날씨가 흐려요.**     It is cloudy.

**Speak like a native with natural expressions**

**It is raining outside.**

밖에 비 와요. 🔊

▸ 눈 와요/눈 내려요 snowing

**Take an umbrella with you.**

우산 가져가세요. 🔊

▸ 챙기세요.

● In this context 가져가세요 and 챙기세요 mean same.

**The heat is killing me.**

더워 죽겠어요. 🔊

▸ 추워 so cold

● When the weather is extremely hot or cold, people say '-아/어 죽겠어요'(meaning "I'm dying") in an exaggerated manner.

**It is sunny today.**

오늘은 날씨가 화창해요. 🔊

▸ 좋아요 nice; good

**A typhoon coming.**

태풍이 온대요. 🔊

**There is a lot of particulate matter.**

미세먼지가 심해요. 🔊

▸ 황사 yellow dust

● During spring, the particulate matter and yellow dust are at very high levels, so take this into consideration if traveling to Korea in the spring.

**It has become chilly.**

공기가 서늘해졌어요. 🔊

▸ 쌀쌀 cold

● Once summer is over, fall starts and the weather becomes chilly, we say '서늘하다'. As winter approaches and it becomes colder, we use '쌀쌀하다'.

**197**

**The temperature difference is quite high.**

일교차가 심해요. 🔊

▷ **커요** big

● '일교차 심하다' and '일교차가 크다' can be used interchangeably.

---

**It is cold, so bundle up.**

추우니까 따뜻하게 입으세요. 🔊
[따뜨타게]

**It snowed a lot.**

눈이 많이 왔어요. 🔊

▷ **비가** rain

Write down the appropriate sentence in the blank space and practice your pronunciations by reading out loud.

**Seohyeon**   **다녀오겠습니다.**
See you.

**Minjun**   **잠깐,** _____ . ❶
Wait, take the umbrella!

**Seohyeon**   **왜요? 지금 비 와요?**
Why? Is it raining now?

**Minjun**   **네, 지금** _____ . ❷
Yes, it's raining outside.

**Seohyeon**   **괜찮아요. 빨리 뛰어가면 돼요.**
It's okay. I can just make a run for it.

**Minjun**   **안 될걸요? 곧** _____ . ❸
That doesn't sound good. A typhoon is coming soon.

**Answer**

❶ Take the umbrella!     우산 가져가세요!
❷ It's raining outside.     밖에 비 와요.
❸ A typhoon is coming.     태풍이 온대요.

TRACK 89

# 지난주에는 진짜 바빴어요.

## I was really busy last week.

  **Do you want to know How to talk about your busy schedule?**

How are you doing? Is your day-to-day life really busy? Presently, most people do seem to be awfully busy. Due to that, the phrase '바쁘다 바빠 현대사회' has become mainstream in Korea. It means 'busy, busy modern society'. It has become quite normal for people to have limited free time due to their busy lifestyles and many expressions have been created to describe this. Let's learn how to talk about your busy schedule in today's lesson.

---

**Today's Pattern**

| N+에는 | 진짜 바빴어요. |
|---|---|
| **지난주에는** | **진짜 바빴어요.** |
| **last week** | **I was really busy** |

**I was really busy last week.**
**~에는 진짜 바빴어요.**

---

**5 Key** **Sentences**

- **지난주에는 진짜 바빴어요.**  I was really busy last week.
- **이번 주에는 진짜 바빴어요.**  I have been really busy this week.
  [이번쭈에는]
- **이번 달에는 진짜 바빴어요.**  I have been really busy all month.
  [이번따레는]
- **이번 학기에는 진짜 바빴어요.**  I've been really busy throughout this semester.
  [이버낙끼에는]
- **지난 학기에는 진짜 바빴어요.**  I was really busy last semester.

**Speak like a native with natural expressions**

**Did you finish all your work?**　일은 다 끝냈어요? ◁ᴷ
[끈내써요]

**My schedule is so packed today as well.**　오늘도 일정이 빡빡해요. ◁ᴷ

● The word '빡빡하다'means that one has no free time at all; not even a few minutes can be carved out.

**It's been really hectic.**　정신없이 바빴어요. ◁ᴷ

● This expression means that you have been so busy you were going out of your mind. It is used quite often in daily conversations.

**I don't even have time to grab a bite.**　밥 먹을 시간도 없어요. ◁ᴷ

**I have a lot of overdue work.**　일이 밀려 있어요. ◁ᴷ

● '밀려 있다' can be used when you have a lot of unfinished tasks or when you have a lot of files piled up in one place.

**I'm bogged down with work.**　일 때문에 꼼짝을 못 해요. ◁ᴷ

● '꼼짝을 못 하다' means not being able to make even the slightest movement. This sentence implies that you have so much work that you really cannot go anywhere.

**I have so much work to do**　할 일이 너무 많아요. ◁ᴷ

▶ **회의가** meeting

**... because of a new project**　　　새로운 프로젝트 때문에요. 🔊

> **시험 공부** exam revision; studying for
> an exam
> **프레젠테이션** presentation
> ● We say 'presentation', 프레젠테이션, when
> there is an important event, such as
> proposing a new business or making an
> announcement at a bidding competition.

**I have to proceed with a**　　　5일 동안 워크숍을 진행해야 돼요. 🔊
**workshop for 5 days.**

> **행사를** event

**I have to finish a proposal by**　　이번 주까지 제안서를 끝내야 돼요. 🔊
**this week.**

Write down the appropriate sentence in the blank space and practice your pronunciations by reading out loud.

Siwoo _____ ? ❶

Are you done with your work?

**Sooah** **아니요. 왜요?**

No. Why?

Siwoo **괜찮으면 주말에 같이 영화 보자고요.**

If you don't mind, let's go to see a movie together on the week-

end.

**Sooah** **죄송해요.** _____ . ❷

I'm sorry. I have too much work to do.

Siwoo **그래도 밥 먹을 시간은 있죠?**

But you still have time to eat, right?

**Sooah** **아니요,** _____ . ❸

No, I don't even have time to eat.

---

**Answer**

❶ Are you done with your work?　일은 다 끝냈어요?
❷ I have too much work to do.　할 일이 너무 많아요.
❸ I don't even have time to eat. 밥 먹을 시간도 없어요.

# 어디에서 만날까?
## Where shall we meet?

TRACK 91

 **Do you want to know How to make an appointment with friends?**

Making plans with your friends is always exciting, especially if it is Korean friend you met recently. In this lesson will cover expressions you would use when you and your friend(s) are deciding where and how to meet, and what you will do when you get together. As these conversations normally take place among friends, we will use 반말 (informal speech)!

---

### Today's **Pattern**

| Ad(where/when) | 만날까? |
|:---:|:---:|
| **어디에서** | **만날까?** |
| **Where** | **shall we meet?** |

**Where shall we meet?**
어디에서/언제/몇 시에 만날까?

---

### 5 Key Sentences ————————————

- **어디에서 만날까?**  Where shall we meet?
- **언제 만날까?**  When shall we meet?
- **무슨 요일에 만날까?**  What day shall we meet?
- **몇 시에 만날까?**  What time shall we meet?
  [며씨에]
- **금요일에 만날까?**  Shall we meet on Friday?

**Speak like a native with natural expressions**

**When are you free?**

언제 시간 돼? 🔊

- The expression '시간이 되다' here means 'to have time'; another way to say it is '시간이 있다'.

**Which day is a good day?**

무슨 요일이 좋아? 🔊

**Do you want to go shopping with me?**

나랑 같이 쇼핑하러 갈래? 🔊

▸ **영화 보러** go to see a movie

**Is there anything you don't like?**

싫어하는 거 있어? 🔊
[시러아능거]

▸ **먹고 싶은** anything you want to eat

**How does 7pm sound?**

저녁 7시 어때? 🔊

▸ **금요일** Friday

**This week doesn't work for me**

이번 주는 안 돼. 🔊

▸ **토요일은** Saturday

**I just arrived.**

방금 도착했어. 🔊

- This expression is used to let your friend(s) know that you have arrived at the meeting location. and Koreans often use the expression '거의 다 왔어' when it's just around the corner.

**Sorry, it seems I'll be a bit late.** 미안한데 조금 늦을 거 같아.

- It is always polite to send a message, like this one, to let your friends know that you will be late because there is traffic or because something came up.

**Just wait 5 minutes for me.** 5분만 기다려 줘.

**It's alright. Take your time.** 괜찮아. 천천히 와.

- This is used when the other party explains that they will unfortunately be late, and you want to let them know that you understand and they shouldn't be worried (However, just because someone tells you to take your time, it doesn't mean you should actually take your time!).

Write down the appropriate sentence in the blank space and practice your pronunciations by reading out loud.

Seohyeon  _____? ❶
Do you want to go shopping with me?

Sooah  그래. _____? ❷
Sure. What day shall we meet?

Seohyeon  **토요일 어때?**
How about Saturday?

Sooah  **좋아.** _____? ❸
All right. Where do you want to meet?

Seohyeon  **음, 코엑스가 좋을 거 같아. 2시 괜찮아?**
Well, I think COEX would be good. Is 2 o'clock okay for you?

Sooah  **응, 토요일 2시에 코엑스, 맞지?**
Yes. At COEX on Saturday at 2, right?

### Answer

❶ Do you want to go shopping with me?  나랑 같이 쇼핑하러 갈래?
❷ What day shall we meet?  무슨 요일에 만날까?
❸ Where do you want to meet?  어디에서 만날까?

TRACK 93

# 요즘 완전 핫하잖아.
## It's really popular these days.

 **Do you want to know How to talk about TV shows/movies?**

Talking about the dramas you like can be really fun. We will learn some expressions that you can use in such conversations. You can use the expression '요즘 완전 V/Adj + 잖아', which means 'It is really V/Adj these days'. The '-잖아' ending can only be used when the person you're speaking to already knows what you are talking about, and it has a 'you know that too, right?' nuance to it. Let's take a closer look at these expressions.

---

**Today's Pattern**

| 요즘 완전 | V/Adj+잖아 |
|---|---|
| **요즘 완전** | **핫하잖아.** |
| now really | It's really like a thing. |

**It's really popular these days.**
요즘 완전 ~잖아.

---

**5 Key** **Sentences**

- **요즘 완전 핫하잖아.**    It's really popular these days.
- **요즘 완전 대세잖아.**    It's a huge trend these days
- **요즘 완전 꽂혔잖아.**    I got all amped on in.
  [꼬쳗짜나]
- **요즘 완전 잘 나가잖아.**    It sells really well these days.
- **요즘 완전 빠졌잖아.**    I am really into it these days.

- 핫하다=인기가 많다 (to be very popular) / 대세 big trend / 꽂히다: a slang that means to be really fixed on something.

**Speak like a native with natural expressions**

**Have you seen Kingdom?**

너 '킹덤' 봤어? 🔊

▸ **오징어 게임** Squid games

**Who starred in it?**

배우 누구 나와? 🔊

● It is more grammatically correct to say '배우는 누가 나와?', but during conversations among friends, it is more common to hear this.

**I am really looking forward to it!**

엄청 기대되는데! 🔊

▸ **완전** really, totally

**Is it that interesting?**

그렇게 재밌어? 🔊

▸ **별로야?** uninteresting, nothing to be excited about

● When talking about a drama that there has been a lot of talk about, you can say '그렇게 OOO?' (where OOO can be replaced by an adjective or verb).

**I haven't seen it yet.**

아직 그거 못 봤어. 🔊

**The plot twist is really shocking.**

반전이 충격적이야. 🔊

**It was really funny.**

진짜 웃겼어. 🔊
[욷껴써]

▸ **연기를 잘했어** the acting was great

**It was moving.** 감동적이었어. 🔊


**It was a bit boring.** 좀 지루했어. 🔊

▷ 재미없었어 boring, uninteresting


**It was to my liking** 내 취향이었어. 🔊

▷ 취향은 아니었어 It was not to my liking

Write down the appropriate sentence in the blank space and practice your pronunciations by reading out loud.

**Sooah**    **너 '이상한 변호사 우영우' 봤어?**

Did you watch 'Extraordinary Attorney Woo'?

**Siwoo**    **당연하지,** _____ . ❶

Of course, it's really popular these days.

**Sooah**    **난 아직 못 봤는데,** _____ ? ❷

I haven't seen it yet, is it that fun?

**Siwoo**    **어! 순수하고 예측 불가하고 감동적이야.**

Oh! It's pure, unpredictable and touching.

**Sooah**    **오,** _____ ! ❸

Oh, I'm really looking forward to it now!

**Siwoo**    **아마 네 취향일걸. 꼭 봐 봐!**

I think it's your type. Make sure to watch it!

### Answer

❶ It's really popular these days.    요즘 완전 핫하잖아.
❷ is it that fun?    그렇게 재밌어?
❸ I'm really looking forward to it now!    완전 기대되는데!

TRACK 95

# 체크카드를 만들고 싶어요.

**I want to get a debit card.**

---

 **Do you want to know How to make a debit card?**

If you come to Korea for a working holiday or teach English on a short-term basis, you have to open a Korean bank account. This would be easier if the bank had an English speaking employee, however, this is unlikely in a smaller local bank. Today, let's learn some expressions to help ease the process of opening a bank account and getting a debit card.

---

### Today's **Pattern**

| N+을/를 | V+고 싶어요 |
|---|---|
| **체크카드를** | **만들고 싶어요.** |
| a debit card | I want to get |

**I want to get a debit card.**
체크카드를 만들고 싶어요.

---

### 5 Key Sentences

- **체크카드를 만들고 싶어요.** — I want to get a debit card.
- **신용카드를 만들고 싶어요.** — I'd like to get a credit card.
  [시뇽카드]
- **예금 계좌를 개설하고 싶어요.** — I'd like to open a savings account
- **잔액을 조회하고 싶어요.** — I want to check my balance.
- **10만원을 송금하고 싶어요.** — I want to transfer 100,000 won.
  [심마눠늘]

**Speak like a native with natural expressions**

**I want to open an installment savings account**

적금 계좌를 개설하려고 하는데요. ◁⟨

▸ 만들려고 create, make

**Can you fill in the application form, please?**

신청서를 작성해 주시겠어요? ◁⟨

● In most banks, you have to fill in an application form to open an account. If there are any words you don't understand, ask the bank staff for the meaning by saying '이건 무슨 뜻이에요?'.

**I forgot my password**

비밀번호를 잊어버렸어요. ◁⟨
[이저버려써요]

**I lost my credit card**

신용카드를 분실했어요. ◁⟨

▸ 잃어버렸어요.
[이러버려써요]

● The words '잊어버리다' [pronounced 이저버리다] and '잃어버리다' [이러버리다] may look similar, but they mean completely different things, depending on how they are pronounced. Be sure to pronounce them correctly.

**When will I receive the card?**

카드는 언제쯤 받을 수 있어요? ◁⟨

● 쯤 about

**It will take about a week**

일주일쯤 걸릴 거예요. ◁⟨

● 걸리다 takes

What is the interest rate?

이자율은 어떻게 돼요? 🔊

Where is the ATM?

ATM은 어디에 있어요? 🔊

- 현금 지급기 = ATM

Please register for an online banking too.

온라인 뱅킹도 등록해 주세요. 🔊

- ▶등록하다 to register

Please send the invoice via text message.

청구서는 문자로 주세요. 🔊

- ▶ 메일로 email
- ▶ 우편으로 letter mail

Write down the appropriate sentence in the blank space and practice your pronunciations by reading out loud.

Dustin _____. ❶

I'd like to get a debit card.

**Bank teller** 신분증 주시겠어요?

May I have your ID, please

Dustin 네, 여기 있어요.

Sure, here you go.

**Bank teller** _____? ❷

Can you fill in the application form?

Dustin 네, 카드는 언제쯤 받을 수 있을까요?

Yes. When can I get the card?

**Bank teller** _____. ❸

It'll take about a week.

**Answer**

❶ I'd like to make a debit card.      체크카드를 만들고 싶어요.
❷ Can you fill out the application form?      신청서를 작성해 주시겠어요?
❸ It'll take about a week.      일주일쯤 걸릴 거예요.

TRACK 97

# 보증금이 얼마예요?

**How much is the deposit?**

 **Do you want to know How to rent a house?**

In Korea, there two ways of renting a house or apartment; 월세 monthly rent and 전세(jeonse); lump-sum housing lease. If you choose to rent a studio apartment on a monthly basis, you would need to pay a deposit between 5 and 30 million won ($3800 - $22800), and then pay a small monthly rent. If you choose to jeonse, you would usually pay a deposit of several hundred million won at the start of your lease, which you'll get back after the end of the lease.

**Today's Pattern**

| N+이/가 | 얼마예요? |
|---|---|
| **보증금이** | **얼마예요?** |
| **the deposit** | **How much is it?** |

**How much is the deposit?**
~이/가 얼마예요?

**5 Key** **Sentences**

- **보증금이 얼마예요?**  How much is the deposit?
- **월세가 얼마예요?**  How much is the monthly rent?
  [월쎄]
- **관리비가 얼마예요?**  How much is the management fee?
  [괄리비]
- **전세로 얼마예요?**  How much is for jeonse?
- **중계 수수료가 얼마예요?**  How much is the agent's fee?

**Speak like a native with natural expressions**

**I'm looking for a studio around Itaewon.**

이태원 근처 원룸을 찾고 있어요. 🔊

▸ **복층을** loft with two floors
▸ **아파트를** apartment

● For reference, a place with two rooms (방) is called a '투룸'. For anything above that, you can ask using the number of rooms and the type of house you want: 방 세 개(네 개…) 짜리+ 아파트 (빌라) 찾고 있어요.

**Is it possible to have a 6 month short term lease?**

6개월 동안 단기 임대가 가능한가요? 🔊

▸ **1년** one year

● The minimum length of stay is usually 2 years, so if you want to rent for less than the standard time, make sure to let your agent know. Short term leases are usually referred to as '단기 임대'.

**It would be great if the apartment was fully-furnished.**

풀옵션이면 좋겠어요. 🔊
[푸롭션]

● The word for 'furnished' is '풀옵션'. This usually means that appliances such as a washing machine, gas range and A.C are already installed.

**How much is the monthly maintenance fee?**

한 달에 관리비는 얼마 정도 나와요? 🔊

▸ **공과금은** utility bill

● Your 공과금 includes all your bills such as the electricity, water, internet and gas bills.

**Does the monthly rent include the maintenance fee?**

월세에 관리비가 포함되나요? 🔊

**Can I move in right away?**

당장 들어갈 수 있나요? 🔊

▸ **언제** when

**How much is the down payment?**

계약금은 얼마예요? 🔊

● To prevent other people from signing a contract for a place you are considering, you can pay some part of the deposit as down payment, usually about 1 million won (approximately 10% to 15% of the deposit).

**A deposit of 10 million won, and a monthly rent of less than 600,000 won.**

보증금 1000만 원에 월 60만 원 이하요. 🔊

● Before starting your house hunting, it is best to set your budget for the deposit and monthly rent.

**I'll live alone**

저 혼자 살 거예요. 🔊

▸ **친구 한 명이랑 같이** with one friend

**Is there a leasing service for foreigners?**

외국인이 아파트를 임대할 수 있는 서비스가 있나요? 🔊

Write down the appropriate sentence in the blank space and practice your pronunciations by reading out loud.

**Mary** _____. ❶

I'm looking for a studio apartment near Hongdae.

**Real estate agent** 그래요, 가격은 얼마로 생각하세요?

Alright, what is your budget?

**Mary** _____. ❷

For deposit, it's 10 million won, and a monthly rent of less than 600,000 won.

**Real estate agent** 여자분 혼자 사실 건가요?

Are you going to live alone?

**Mary** 네, _____. ❸

Yes, I'm going to live alone.

**Real estate agent** 알겠어요. 한 번 찾아볼 테니까 기다리세요.

All right. I'll look for it, please wait.

**Answer**

❶ I'm looking for a studio apartment near Hongdae.
홍대 근처 원룸을 찾고 있어요.

❷ For deposit, it's 10 million won, and a monthly rent of less than 600,000 won.
보증금 1000만 원에 월 60만 원 이하요.

❸ I'm going to live alone. 저 혼자 살 거예요.

# 미국까지 얼마나 걸릴까요?
## How long will it take to reach America?

 **Do you want to know How to send a package?**

Foreigners who stay in Korea for a year or more might be sending a package or more abroad at least once during their stay. They could be sending presents to their family or they might be sending their belongings back in preparation for their return home. When sending mail or packages abroad, most people in Korea use the post office. Today, let's go over some expressions you can use when mailing packages at the post office.

---

**Today's Pattern**

| N+까지(N+로/으로) | 얼마나 걸릴까요? |
|---|---|
| **미국까지** | **얼마나 걸릴까요?** |
| to America | How long will it take |

**How long will it take to reach America?**
~까지/~로/~으로 얼마나 걸릴까요?

---

**5 Key** **Sentences**

- **미국까지 얼마나 걸릴까요?** — How long will it take to reach America?
- **항공편으로 얼마나 걸릴까요?** — How long will it take if sent by air?
- **배로 얼마나 걸릴까요?** — How long will it take by sea?
  배 ship
- **특송으로 얼마나 걸릴까요?** — How long will an express mail take?
- **일반 우편으로 얼마나 걸릴까요?** — How long will regular mail take?

**Speak like a native with natural expressions**

**Give me a number 3 sized box, please.**

3호 박스 하나 주세요. ◁⠀
[사모 빡스]

- You can buy package boxes with different sizes at the post office. There are boxes from size 1 to size 5 for you to choose from. Things like packing tape, scissors, and paper for packing fragile items can be used for free.

**I would like to send this to the US.**

이거 미국으로 보내고 싶어요. ◁⠀

**Will you be buying insurance?**

보험에 가입하실 건가요? ◁⠀

**How long will it take by EMS?**

EMS로 보내면 얼마예요? ◁⠀

▷ **일반 소포로** regular mail

- EMS, short for Express Mail Service, is a postal service that allows you to send urgent letters, documents or parcels abroad in the fastest and safest way. It is very fast and lets you track your package, but the downside is that it is very expensive.

**What are the contents of your package?**

내용물이 뭐예요? ◁⠀

- Another similar question that you might hear, is '안에 뭐 들었어요?' (literally 'what is inside?').

**Packages over 30kg cannot be shipped.**

**30Kg이 넘으면 배송이 불가능합니다.** 🔊

- In Korea, the kilogram (kg) is the unit for measuring weight. Before packing the parcel to be sent, make sure you check the maximum weight and volume, and the prohibited items when shipping to your desired country. If you go to post it without checking, your package may be rejected.

**Are there any fragile items inside?**

**깨지는 물건은 없나요?** 🔊

**How long will it take to arrive?**

**도착하는 데 얼마나 걸려요?** 🔊

**Will it arrive before Christmas?**

**크리스마스 전까지 도착하나요?** 🔊

**It will take about 2 weeks.**

**한 2주일 정도 걸려요.** 🔊

▶ **약** about
- 한=약 about

Write down the appropriate sentence in the blank space and practice your pronunciations by reading out loud.

| | |
|---|---|
| **Mary** | **이거 미국으로 부치고 싶어요.** |
| | I'd like to mail this to America. |
| Post office worker | 네, _____? ❶ |
| | Sure. What are the contents of your package? |
| **Mary** | **옷이랑 기념품이요.** |
| | Clothes and souvenirs. |
| Post office worker | **일반 소포로 보내 드릴까요?** |
| | Do you mean regular package here? |
| **Mary** | 네, _____? ❷ |
| | Yes, how long will it take to reach America? |
| Post office worker | _____. ❸ |
| | It takes about two weeks. |

**Answer**

❶ What are the contents of your package?  내용물이 뭐예요?
❷ How long will it take to reach America?  미국까지 얼마나 걸릴까요?
❸ It takes about two weeks.  약 2주일 정도 걸려요.

# Organic Korean for upper beginners

**초 판 발 행** 1st edition published 2022. 9. 26

**지 은 이** Written by 서현실 Hyun-Sil Seo
**번 역** Translated by 아모개 에지케 Amoge Ezike
**교정 · 교열** Proofreading by 라즈비 프리야 로버트 Rajvi Priya Robert, 크리스 브라우닝 Chris Browning
**감 수** Editing 김은지 Eun-ji Kim, 이신애 Shin-Ae Lee
**디 자 인** Design by 제이로드(크몽) JLORD (https://blog.naver.com/juliadesign)
**삽 화** Illustrated by @vnvnii
**녹 음** Voice recording by 서현실 Hyun-Sil Seo, 조건 Gun Cho, 엔조 포지아리니 Enzo Forgiarini
**카피라이터** Copywrite by 크리스 브라우닝 Chris Browning
**마 케 팅** Marketing by 모니카 올리비아 밥티스타 Monica A. Oliveira Boptista
**펴 낸 곳** Published by 알파 코리안 클래스 Alpha Korean Class

**주 소** Address 22174인천광역시 미추홀구 제물량로 24번길 33, 102동 1104호
22174 102dong 1104ho, 33, Jemullyang-ro, 24beon-gil, Michuhol-gu, Incheon
**전 화** Telephone +82+70-4046-3222
**팩 스** Fax +82+70-8615-6072
**이 메 일** E-mail support@alphakoreanclass.com

**ISBN** 9798353106456

Made in United States
Troutdale, OR
03/19/2024

18583838R00126